Breed Standard for the Yorkshire Terrier

HINDQUARTERS

Legs quite straight when viewed from behind, moderate turn of stifle. Well covered with hair of rich golden tan a few shades lighter at ends than at roots, not extending higher on hindlegs than stifles.

COAT

Hair on body moderately long, perfectly straight (not wavy), glossy, fine silky texture, not woolly. Fall on head long, rich golden tan, deeper in color at sides of head, about ear roots and on muzzle where it should be very long. Tan on head not to extend on to neck, nor must any sooty or dark hair intermingle with any of tan.

TAIL

Customarily docked to medium length with plenty of hair, darker blue in colour than rest of body, especially at the end of tail. Carried a little higher than level of back.

COLOUR

Dark steel blue (not silver blue), extending from occiput to root of tail, never mingled with fawn, bronze or dark hairs. Hair on chest rich, bright tan. All tan hair darker at the roots than in middle, shading to still lighter at tips.

FEET

Round; nails black.

Photo credits:

Norvia Behling
Carolina Biological Supply
Liza Clancy
Doskocil
Isabelle Francais
James Hayden-Yoav
James R. Hayden, RBP
Carol Ann Johnson

Dwight R. Kuhn
Dr. Dennis Kunkel
Mikki Pet Products
Alice Pantfoeder
Phototake
Jean Claude Revy
C. James Webb

Illustrations by Renée Low

DISTRIBUTED BY:
INTERPET
PUBLISHING
Vincent Lane, Dorking, Surrey RH4 3YX England

Yorkshire Terrier

$\diamond$

by Rachel Keyes

Table of Contents

ISBN: 978-0-96685-926-3

History of the Yorkshire Terrier

Whilst the Industrial Revolution lead most of the world toward pursuing the bigger and better, some brilliant engineers sought smaller and better. The Yorkshire Terrier is a remarkable man-made creation of the mid-nineteenth century, at a time when British dog enthusiasts were crossing many types of terriers in order to develop dogs handsomely suited for their needs. In the counties of Yorkshire and Lancashire, the breed we now know as the

The Yorkshire Terrier is a unique British creation and is counted amongst the world's most popular dogs.

The English Toy Terrier (Black and Tan), also known as the Toy Manchester Terrier, may have been in the family tree of the Yorkshire Terrier.

The Maltese, with its long, flowing hair, may be a Yorkshire Terrier ancestor.

The Skye Terrier, although significantly larger than the Yorkie, is thought to be in the breed's bloodlines, possibly contributing some unique colour genes.

10

smaller than the Skye Terrier and shorter in back, with grey colouration and a rougher coat. The Clydesdale Terrier also bore resemblance to the Skye Terrier of today, with the characteristic well feathered prick ears, a floor-length coat in dark blue with tan markings on the face, legs and feet, and a long body. Both the Clydesdale and the Paisley were formidable ratters, used by miners

Yorkshire Terrier emerged in its most recognisable form. The first shows for toy terriers in Great Britain began in 1860, and 'Yorkshires' from these two textile counties were counted amongst the first ribbon holders.

Which breeds contributed to the composition of the Yorkshire Terrier, however, is still a great debate. Amongst the contenders are the English Toy Terrier, Maltese, Skye Terrier, Dandie Dinmont Terrier and two extinct breeds known as the Paisley Terrier and the Clydesdale Terrier. The Paisley Terrier is described as

to kill rats down in the shafts that interfered with their work. The Clydesdale, Paisley and Skye Terriers receive credit for the Yorkshire Terrier's length of coat; the Maltese for coat and the diminutive size; and the black and tan Manchester (English Toy Terrier) for colouration. The silken texture of the Yorkie's coat could have come from all the longer coated dogs in the mixture, even though the Paisley and Clydesdale were usually rough coated. Whenever silky-coated puppies occurred in a Paisley or Clydesdale litter, they were discarded until a fad for silky coats began. Both these rough-coated terriers lost favour and the numbers began to diminish significantly.

The extinct Clydesdale Terrier bore a resemblance to the Yorkshire Terrier and may be an ancestor. This breed became absorbed into the other British terrier breeds.

Although our Yorkshire Terriers today are cherished as show dogs and companion animals, there is more than a little fighting spirit in their blood. The English Toy Terriers that were incorporated into the early stock were fierce ratters, working side by side with the miners killing off the vermin, with neither fear nor sympathy towards their prey. These dogs not only killed rats for employment, they did so for entertainment as well. Toward the end of the nineteenth century, rat-killing contests became very popular. The small black and tan terriers, with their smooth coats and fiery temperaments, proved very adept at the quick-fire killing of their ratine foes. Judged against the clock, the dogs had to kill as many rats as possible in a given time frame. Some dogs were able to slay a couple hundred rats in a mere ten-minute time frame! The blood-splattering excitement and the heinous squealing of the rats made this gambling-man's

entertainment as popular as many other 'sports,' including bull-baiting, cockfighting, and dog fighting.

From Manchester, England, Peter Eden has been hailed, perhaps erroneously, as the main 'manufacturer' of the Yorkshire Terrier, even before the breed acquired that name. Eden was not only an expert breeder of Pugs and Bulldogs but also a top dog show judge. His key stud dog was named Albert, who won many prizes at the shows as a young dog. Albert, the first name in The

The modern Yorkshire Terrier is a placid lap dog in most cases. Their ratting days are over, as modern Yorkies are smaller than their ancestors.

11

DID YOU KNOW?

Dogs and wolves are members of the genus *Canis*. Wolves are known scientifically as *Canis lupus* while dogs are known as *Canis domesticus*. Dogs and wolves are known to interbreed. The term canine derives from the Latin derived word *Canis*. The term dog has no scientific basis but has been used for thousands of years. The origin of the word dog has never been authoritatively ascertained.

Kennel Club Stud Book as a Yorkshire Terrier, competed as a Broken-haired, Scotch and Yorkshire Terrier. Eden's influence on the breed was, without a doubt, considerable, though he probably was not the true 'engineer' of the Yorkshire Terrier. It is said that he purchased dogs from the men of Yorkshire and used them in his programme. We are certain that he was a master breeder. Mr. Eden's dogs were amongst the first to possess the desirable blue silky coats marked with mahogany colouration on the head and legs, and a characteristic tuft of hair on the head to drape over the eyes. In fact, Mr. Eden's great dog Albert appears in Huddersfield Ben's pedigree many times on both sides, being twice a great-great-grandfather!

Although Mr. Eden enjoys the credit for engineering the

Yorkshire breed, he does not receive more accolades than Mrs. M. A. Foster for showing and winning in the show ring. Mrs. Foster purchased Huddersfield Ben and exhibited him enthusiastically as well as the other dogs she bred herself. Ben won nearly a hundred prizes attached to Mrs. Foster's lead. Another of Mrs. Foster's top dogs was known as Champion Ted, the winner of nearly 300 awards. He weighed in at a five pounds and was the number-one Yorkie for six years. He was whelped in June 1883. Not surprisingly, he was the progeny of Ben and in his day was unsurpassed as a sire. Mrs. Foster promoted the breed by winning glamourously in the show ring and placing promising puppies in the hands of enthusiastic newcomers to the show scene. Mrs. Foster did for the Yorkshire Terrier breed, back in the 1860s, what we can only hope prominent breeders do for new owners today: encourage and guide new fanciers in the breed,

An early 20th century Yorkshire Terrier, Mrs. M. A. White's dog called Sensation, was considered a model for the breed.

Very popular Yorkies in 1903 were Mr. C. E. Firmstone's dogs: from left to right, Mynd Damaris, Mynd Idol and The Grand Duke.

teach responsibility and proper care. Mrs. Foster raised her Yorkshire Terriers with the utmost care, showed the dogs in top condition, and only exhibited the desirably typey dogs. Unlike many exhibitors today who will enter the ring with a second-rate dog, Mrs. Foster blazed trails for the Yorkshire Terrier breed. She was never seen promoting an inferior dog. Additionally, she was the first woman to be invited to judge a dog show. This occurred in 1889. Although her prowess in the sport was well known, it was previously unheard of for a woman to serve in this prestigious capacity.

At this point in the development of the breed, the set weight of the dogs was around 8 to 10 pounds, significantly reduced from the original size of up to 15 pounds. These smaller dogs, typical of the ones bred by Mr.

Eden and Mrs. Foster, represent the trend that the breed would take over its first few decades. The Victorian sensibility for the petite and beautiful had a lasting effect on the breed, and full-grown dogs would eventually weigh in at around two and a half to three pounds!

Ch. Victoria, bred by Mrs. A. Swan, was born in July 1932 and won many awards including eight Challenge Certificates.

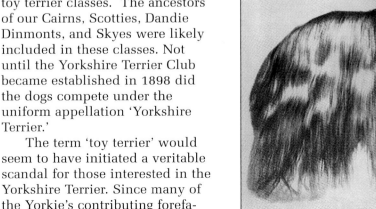

AH, POSTERITY!

The only known photograph of the great Huddersfield Ben appears in the first book on the breed, cleverly titled The Yorkshire Terrier, authored by Sam Jessop. It is a most unflattering portrait of this prepotent sire and grand little gentleman. It was taken after his death, fully mounted by a taxidermist.

While the first dog show, in 1859, at Newcastle-on Tyne, only offered classes for sporting dogs (pointers and setters), the show at Birmingham the following year included toy terriers. Birmingham, by the way, is the present location of the country's most prestigious and oldest show, the Crufts Dog Show. 'Yorkshires,' though not by name, were present at the show. 'Scotch' or 'Broken-haired Terriers' were the names usually applied to dogs in these toy terrier classes. The ancestors of our Cairns, Scotties, Dandie Dinmonts, and Skyes were likely included in these classes. Not until the Yorkshire Terrier Club became established in 1898 did the dogs compete under the uniform appellation 'Yorkshire Terrier.'

The term 'toy terrier' would seem to have initiated a veritable scandal for those interested in the Yorkshire Terrier. Since many of the Yorkie's contributing forefa-

Ch. Tinker of Glendinan as he appeared during the Kennel Club Show held in 1933.

thers were rough-and-tumble, rough-coated terriers, certain fanciers preferred the Yorkshire to be a true working terrier. The other camp, affected by their Victorian ideals, sought a diminutive silky-coated dog, suitable for warming one's lap instead of exterminating one's stables. This camp desired a toy dog, not a terrier! Some dedicated Yorkshiremen, well known as industrious and clever dogmen, wanted a competent rat-killer that was also attractive. Thus, the first batch of 'Yorkshire pudding' was whipped up, crossing the talented and fearless Broken-haired terriers with the smaller and somewhat unusual Clydesdale, no less undaunted in the rat pits. There is no doubt that it took many additions to the recipe, at least six different terrier types, to finally reach the desirable, dutiful Yorkshire Terrier—-a diminutive charmer in blue and bronze capable of the task at hand. It would seem that the long coat of the Yorkshire Terrier would interfere with the task of killing rats underground. Not necessarily, as some historians purport that the long coat gave the miners something to grab onto to pull the dog out of the ground. As the Yorkshire Terrier developed, the controversy between terrier and toy faded, since many workers decided that the Yorkshire was an excellent worker, despite its fancy appearance. Today the breed is still the hearty little terrier, though his sweet personable character has become his hallmark claim to fame. The Yorkshire's ability to warm his owner's home, in modern times, certainly outclasses his ability to keep it vermin-free.

Lady Edith Windham-Dawson

DID YOU KNOW?
Since dogs have been inbred for centuries, their physical and mental characteristics are constantly being changed to suit man's desires for hunting, retrieving, scenting, guarding, and warming their master's laps. During the past 150 years, dogs have been judged according to physical characteristics as well as functional abilities. Few breeds can boast a genuine balance between physique, working ability and temperament.

A coat that was hard to beat was bred by Mrs. A. Swan, 1932.

Charming, one of Lady Windham's great champions, during the 1930s.

WHAT'S IN A NAME?
The word terrier in Yorkshire Terrier has real meaning. The early members of the breed were terrific ratters. Admittedly these early Yorkies weighed in at around 14 pounds, compared to the wee 5-pound dogs we cherish today.

Ch. Rose of the World, a typical champion Yorkshire Terrier of the 1932 season, as she appeared at the Ladies Kennel Association.

followed in the footsteps of the great Mrs. Foster. Lady Windham was both a breeder of top Yorkshire Terriers and show judge beginning in the 1930s. Dogs

MURDER BY THE DOZEN.

In the rat pits, Yorkies were used by kill rats against the clock. Amongst the great Yorkshire Terriers who excelled in the rat contests was Huddersfield Ben, one of the most important early Yorkshire Terriers, the sire of many champions. He died in 1871. Ben was bred by W. Eastwood of Huddersfield and later sold to Mrs. Jonas Foster of Bradford.

bearing Lady Windham's kennel name, Soham, won many ribbons in Great Britain and Ireland.

The Yorkshire Terrier was amongst the first breeds recognised by the newly formed Kennel Club in 1873. A quarter century passed, however, before the breed's official standard was drafted. Established in 1898, the Yorkshire Terrier Club formed in order to write a standard for the breed. A breed standard is a written description of what the ideal specimen of that breed should look like. It is used by breeders and judges as a guide for evaluating dogs in the show ring and therefore in breeding programmes. The breed standard, drafted by the parent club, is then accepted and adopted by the national kennel club. The original breed standard, drafted in 1898, remained in force until 1950. The changing trends in the breed, fired by controversy over correct and desirable colouration and the thriving popularity of the breed, brought about revisions to the standard (mostly concerning the dark, steel blue colouration, not silver).

THE YORKSHIRE TERRIER IN THE U.S.
The first blue and tan to be heralded in the land of the red, white and blue was Belle, a bitch whelped in 1877, owned by Mr. A. E. Godeffroy. Belle was

EARLY YORKIE FANCIERS WERE FAKERS!
Before the establishment of The Kennel Club, breeding and showing dogs was a fairly profitable undertaking. Unscrupulous exhibitors 'faked' their way to the winner's circle many times, by 'painting' their dogs' coats with colouring agents, lying about a dog's age, and surgically 'correcting' any unattractive attributes. Some things never change, but now there are penalties!

registered before the American Kennel Club was formed, in a ledger belonging to A. N. Rouse. Two other early imports, amongst the first in the AKC stud book, were known as Jim and Rose, both derived from Scottish breeding and were owned by J. A. Nickerson and R. R. Bushell of Boston, Massachusetts.

Ch. Mendham Billy in a 1933 photo which demonstrates how the fall beard should be rolled and tied.

YORKIE EXPERT AND WOMEN'S LIBBER
Prominent Yorkie breeder and exhibitor, Mrs. Jonas Foster was the first woman ever to judge a dog show. The year was 1889, when the Women's Movement was well under way.

WHO'S AFRAID OF THE BIG BAD MOUSE!

If you have ever known a Yorkshire Terrier, there is little doubt that this toy dog knows well his fearless, animated ancestors. While he is considerably too small to take on a full-grown rat (that could easily outweigh him), he is more than willing to do battle with a mouse.

The breed became established in the U.S. through the efforts of many dedicated breeders on both coasts and dogs were exhibited at many of the country's most presti-gious shows. Strong classes of the little blue and tan dogs impressed many influential judges in the fancy.

By the 1950s, the breed became remarkably popular, and show dogs par excellence swept the national shows. Many of these great dogs bore the kennel prefix Wilweir, owned by Janet Bennet and Joan Gordon. The Yorkshire Terrier Club of America was accepted by the AKC in 1958. The club revised The Kennel Club standard, which was approved by AKC in 1966.

THE LONG ROAD TO VICTORY

The Westminster Kennel Club Dog

An Irish Yorkshire Terrier named Little Pickwick was owned by Miss Sally Logan of Belfast. At the 1931 Navan Dog Show, held in County Meath, Ireland, it won First Any Variety Toy, First Any Variety Terrier, First Yorkshire Terrier and Best Yorkshire in Show.

Show, held annually since 1877, is the oldest dog show in the world. This unique American event, second only to the Kentucky Derby as oldest sporting event in the U.S., attracts 2,500 dogs each year at Madison Square Garden in New York City. Although 14 years older, this event is not nearly as large as the Crufts Dog Show though equally prestigious.

Only one Yorkshire Terrier has ever won Westminster, and it took the breed over 100 years to

One of Mrs. Swan's best examples (1933) of a Yorkshire Terrier.

do so: Ch. Cede Higgins, owned by Barbara and Charles Switzer, claimed top honours in 1978.

According to *Hutchinson's Encyclopedia*, published in the 1930s, 'A Yorkshire Terrier's coat needs cultivating with extreme care, especially the full beard and moustaches, which should never be left untied. Coats that trail the ground should be rolled in paper and securely tied to allow the dog maximum freedom of movement.'

Why the Yorkshire Terrier?

THE JOY OF LOVING A YORKIE
Who can resist the charms of a teacup full of Yorkshire Terrier? What could shake the blues from your afternoon tea more readily than a blue and tan toy terrier? It would appear that most anyone inclined to own a Yorkshire Terrier should do so! There are so many gigantic advantages wrapped up in this smallest of British terriers.

Given the tiny size of the breed, the Yorkshire does not impose upon your space. You do not need a palatial estate with a top-security fence. You do not need a large home to provide ample exercise for the dog indoors. You do not need to stress your budget to afford to feed the dog. You do not need to purchase expensive equipment to train, house, and otherwise accommodate the Yorkshire Terrier.

You do need to open your heart to this three-pound wonder and learn to give yourself freely and without reservation to another living creature.

The Yorkshire Terrier welcomes everyone into his world. He is a trusting soul, who shares his affectionate ways with anyone kind and good-humoured enough to spend time with him. Yorkies like people most of all. Whilst they get on with most other dogs, they are not clannish or selfish. Owners are advised to supervise the introduction of their Yorkies to larger dogs. Even though your Yorkie will not be afraid of a larger dog, such as a Dobermann or German Shepherd, the larger dog may not realise his own strength. Many Yorkies have been harmed by larger dogs that playfully mouthed them or pawed down at them. Once the larger dog realises that the Yorkshire Terrier is a

(opposite page) Yorkshire Terriers are so popular now because they are beautiful, small and intelligent. They are like living dolls...but unlike a doll, a dog needs constant care and attention. If you are not prepared to properly care for the Yorkie, you should not get one.

The Yorkshire Terrier is the smallest of the British terriers, though Australia has an even smaller breed.

A MATTER OF SIZE!

While the Yorkshire Terrier may be smaller than what the world commonly thinks of as a dog, he is nonetheless completely dog. The Yorkshire Terrier thinks and acts like every other canine. He interacts with other dogs the same as any other dog. Any other dogs react to him in a thoroughly canine way. Dogs do not perceive size the way humans perceive size. A pint-sized Yorkshire Terrier does not look upon a Basset Hound, Great Dane or Greyhound in awe of its greater size. For the Yorkie's size, he is a giant—-a full-size ambassador of good will, confident and regal.

not vindictive, despite their serious ways in serious times. Like most toy dogs, play is a way of life! Simple games, such as rolling a ball, chasing a string, fetching a bone, etc., make the Yorkie a happy fellow to have about. His extroverted personality, coupled with his playful air, make him an ideal choice for young and old alike. Jumping about the furniture and leaping after imaginary mice and other foes, the Yorkshire Terrier can entertain even the drollest of guests.

Children and the Yorkie are natural comrades. Given the petite size of the Yorkie, caution is in order. Most breeders recommend

Though Yorkies are not truly watch dogs or guard dogs, they are extremely protective of their home and human family.

member of his canine clan, he will want to 'talk dog' with the Yorkie, unaware of the Yorkie's gentile status.

Although not the size of a guard dog, the Yorkshire Terrier is most protective of his home and people. He still possesses all the fire of his terrier ancestors—-he is fearless beyond his grammes. A Yorkshire Terrier, whose temper is incited, will make quite a display of spit and attitude when protecting his owner's property, car, or garden. Yorkies have the memory of elephants! Once you cross a Yorkie and he brands you a foe, he will never forget your transgressions.

For the most part, Yorkies love to have great fun. They are

In short, the Yorkshire Terrier is perfect for someone who wants a small breed that is full of pep, vigour, beauty and love.

that larger Yorkies (even in excess of the seven-pound limit) be selected for families with children. Since young people tend to be pretty rough on their toys (and toy dogs), children must be taught that the Yorkie is a fragile living creature. This is not a Beanie Baby® that can be tossed about with abandon, though admittedly the Yorkie is

as adorable and as collectable! The Yorkshire Terriers can be injured by excitable children who poke at their eyes or tear a ligament or break a leg by tossing or dropping the young dog. Yorkies have much to teach children in terms of care, trust and mutual affection. When properly instructed and supervised, this is a marvellous pairing.

The elderly also adore the Yorkshire Terrier. Their entertaining antics and gentle ways make them suitable for the housebound and those less likely to take their dogs jogging on the oceanfront. Yorkies can receive ample exercise indoors, with an occasional romp through the garden. They are ideal for apartment dwellers or others living in small flats without much access to the outdoors.

When the Yorkshire Terrier is given access to the Great Outdoors, however, he takes to it with zeal. He is a terrier, after all, and the word terrier derives from the Latin word for 'earth'. Yorkies love to play in the grass. They are talented diggers, you can be certain. The breed welcomes all the sporting games of the larger terriers. Athough the Yorkie has neither the poundage of the Dandie Dinmont nor the legginess of the Airedale, the game and pluck of his terrier ancestors still race through his blue arteries.

Children and Yorkies are made to order for each other, though children must be warned that the small Yorkie is a delicate living creature that must be treated with care.

Most Yorkshire Terrier owners admit that being possessed by a Yorkshire Terrier is infectious. Yorkies are not great family dogs, they are family! Owners consider their Yorkies to be a part of the family, like any other child in the household. Given the Yorkie's size and the giant size of his heart and character, it is no surprise that owners depend on their Yorkies for companionship and affection. Thus, many true Yorkie fanciers build a whole family of Yorkies. While most breeders will

THE DELECTABLE, COLLECTABLE YORKSHIRE

Since the Yorkie does not require much space in one's home, owners have a tendency to 'stock up' on them. It is very common for Yorkie enthusiasts to adopt two, three or even a dozen Yorkies! The love and companionship that a single Yorkie can bring to an owner is multiplied and compounded daily with a whole collection of blue and tan babies!

discuss their kennel plans, it is rare to hear a Yorkie breeder talk about a 'kennel.' The Yorkshire is a home buddy, always living amidst the family, totally immersed and involved in the family's day to day routine.

The Yorkie is a family dog. If you like flowers, he will like flowers, too. If you want to walk, he will walk with you. If you want to sleep, he will only be too happy to sleep with you. This personality has won the hearts of many dog owners.

Yorkies thrive on the family's schedule. They instinctively know who comes home first, and they likewise know when someone is late or missing. This family dog cannot sleep if one of his beloved is still not home where he or she belongs. While the Yorkie counts his master or mistress first (like all dogs, the one who feeds and cares for them receives special consideration), every member of the family is regarded in the highest esteem.

A word of caution to the overzealous Yorkie lover: You must resist your primal urge to spoil your Yorkshire Terrier beyond reason. Any overly pampered dog can become difficult to live with. Considering this toy terrier's spirit and determination, once a Yorkie thinks he has his way in all matters of the household, he may become less of a

25

It's easy to want to spoil your Yorkie, but don't give in! They require polite, kind attention without your accommodating their every wish.

joy to have around. By nature, the Yorkie is not a selfish, greedy dog; he is not a stingy eater and does not gorge himself; he does not hide his toys from his play-mates and is quite happy to share his things. Once your obsession has tinkered with this delightful personality, your Yorkie may not be the generous, open-hearted angel you fell in love with.

Be careful. Many 'Yorkie-a-holics,' amongst whom the author might be counted, have embarrassing stories about the extents to which they go to spoil their adorable little friends.

The Yorkie is a lot of personality in a little dog.

Although this fancier has never resorted to anything like this, I have heard of Yorkie owners who have purchased cradles and highchairs for their Yorkies; who visit the butcher daily to furnish top-grade dinner meat; who have cancelled holiday plans if the six Yorkies were not invited; who have knitted and crocheted sweaters and booties for their dogs; and who have given up highly successful careers in the business world to stay home with their Yorkies (and freelance write about her favourite subject?!).

If you find yourself falling into any of the above categories, then you will fit in well with the wonderfully dedicated, delicate-ly balanced world of Yorkshire Terrier ownership. Welcome!

Many owners of Yorkies do not stop at just one. It is not uncommon for a dog lover to buy more than one Yorkie; they're addictive!

BREED-SPECIFIC HEALTH CONCERNS OF THE YORKSHIRE TERRIER

Your Yorkie's eyes are not only a good indication of his affection and devotion for you, his owner, but an excellent way of evaluating the dog's health. As in all dogs, the eyes should be clear and bright, a general sign of good health and nutrition. Look for any cloudiness or opacity in the eyes of your dog, this could indicate a problem to bring to your veterinary surgeon's attention.

With the Yorkshire Terrier, however, the breed is prone to some hereditary eye conditions. Amongst these conditions, the most common are cataracts, progressive retinal atrophy, keratoconjunctivitis sicca, and ulcerative keratitis.

Yorkies develop cataracts after three years of age, most frequently between three and six years. Fortunately veterinary advances make it possible for successful cataract surgery to take place. As in humans, the cataracts can be

Yorkie owners should pay special attention to their dogs' eyes. Any sign of cloudiness in the eye is reason to visit the vet.

removed by a trained surgeon. Since the condition is considered hereditary, dogs with cataracts should be excluded from the breeding programme.

Progressive retinal atrophy, abbreviated PRA, causes blindness in affected dogs. Commonly, the Yorkshire Terrier is struck by PRA in the later years, usually around eight years of age, though it can be as early as five and as late as twelve. As the name describes, the deterioration of the retina is progressive. Affected dogs experience limitations in their sight, but since Yorkies are very adaptive, the owner may not notice that the dog's sight is failing. Usually, PRA has become pretty severe by the time the owner is aware that the dog is affected.

Keratoconjunctivitis sicca is abbreviated KCS and is more commonly called 'dry eye.' The

Make sure your Yorkie's eyes are clear and bright, without any sign of mucous.

'dry eye' condition results from the lacrimal glands' failure to produce tears in the eye. The cornea suffers from lack of 'wetness' and these dry areas cause damage to the eye. Mucous accumulation around the eyes indicates to the owner that there is a problem with the eye. Treatment is available which includes antibiotics and other drugs. In unusual cases, surgery can correct the condition. Like PRA, KCS is hereditary and affected dogs should not be bred.

The eyes of the Yorkie are a weak point. If you have regular veterinary care, your vet should be able to diagnose the problem at its onset and keep your Yorkie as healthy as he is beautiful.

29

KCS (keratoconjunctivitis sicca) or dry eye is the result of the failure of the lachrymal glands and the eyes don't tear. Dogs don't produce tears when they cry or whine. Tears are produced to keep the eye moist and to flush away foreign particles that lodge in the eye.

The fourth eye condition affecting the Yorkie, ulcerative keratitis also affects the cornea. Infection and ulceration (formation of ulcers) on the cornea are caused by the dog's hair's irritating its eyes. Owners may notice their Yorkies blinking excessively, pawing at their eyes from discomfort, and a watery appearance to the eye. This is not a hereditary condition but merely a result of the Yorkshire Terrier's

Yorkies have prominent eyes that are susceptible to irritation. Keeping the dog's eye area free of excess hair can prevent a problem.

prominent eyes. The condition can be treated with antibiotics and special applications.

Two orthopaedic conditions that commonly affect toy dogs and other small breeds are Legg-Calve-Perthes disease and patellar luxation. Commonly seen in young Yorkies, LCP has a high incidence in the breed. The disease causes lameness in the hip joint,

While you cannot predict your Yorkie's health, you can give him an advantage by practising preventative medicine.

CONTACT LENSES FOR YOUR YORKIE!

Does your Yorkshire Terrier need contact lenses?! Yes, some Yorkies affected with severe cases of ulcerative keratitis are fitted with contact lenses. Unlike in humans, these lenses do not correct the vision, but they do protect the dog's lens from any irritating fur, which cause the ulcers on the eyes.

is commonly recommended before the condition causes arthritis.

Von Willebrand's disease (vWD) is a congenital disease seen in many breeds of dog. VWD is a bleeding disorder. Unfortunately, the disease is becoming of increasing impor-

resulting from the collapsing of the femoral head of the leg. Very frequently, in eight or nine out of ten cases, only one leg is affected. It is likely hereditary, though veterinary research is not conclusive. Patellar luxation, in layperson's terms, means a 'slipped kneecap.' Although it is hereditary, it is not usually a serious problem. Cases vary greatly depending on the laxity of the patellar. In young dogs, surgery

HONKING: A SIGNAL

Honking, hacking Yorkies should signal concern in owners. A honking cough from a Yorkshire Terrier, particularly around seven or eight years of age, often accompanied by obesity, often indicates a collapsed trachea. The honking attacks are aggravated by stress. The condition can be treated, but weight loss and stress management are mandatory.

31

The present and future health of your Yorkshire Terrier depends upon the frequency of visitation and competency of your selected veterinary surgeon.

tance to the Yorkshire Terrier. Breeders and vets have noted a large number of cases in recent times, particularly in dogs over five years of age. Not all dogs with vWD are diagnosed, depending on the level of clotting. Some dogs are not diagnosed until a problem presents itself in surgery (spaying and neutering procedures most commonly). Depending on the level of clotting factor, the dog may or may not be badly affected. No Yorkie with vWD should be included in a breeder's programme.

In all, the Yorkshire Terrier is a healthy, adaptable dog. Owners are well advised to investigate each of the above-mentioned disorders and to discuss them with the vet. The better informed an owner is, the longer will be the life of his Yorkie.

Your Yorkie depends upon you for food, shelter and health care. If you are unable or unwilling to supply these three essentials, you should reconsider bringing a Yorkie into your life.

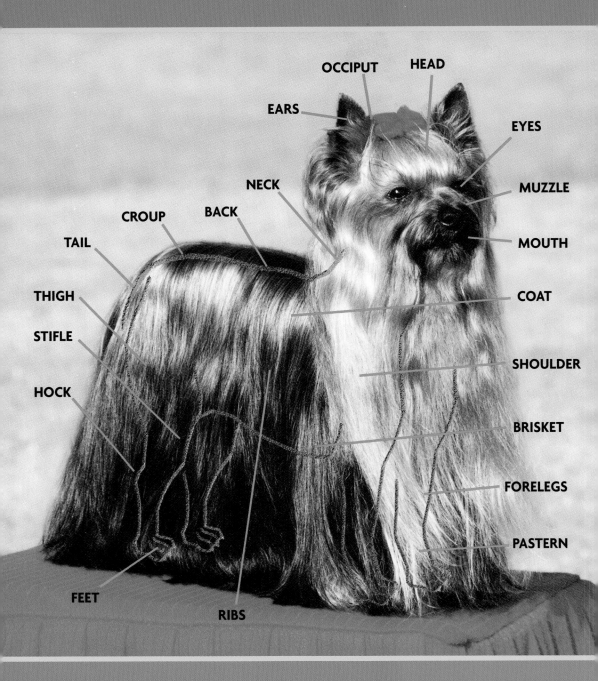

OCCIPUT

HEAD

EARS

EYES

NECK

MUZZLE

CROUP

BACK

MOUTH

TAIL

COAT

THIGH

STIFLE

SHOULDER

HOCK

BRISKET

FORELEGS

PASTERN

FEET

RIBS

Breed Standard for the Yorkshire Terrier

THE KENNEL CLUB STANDARD FOR THE YORKSHIRE TERRIER

General Appearance: Long-coated, coat hanging quite straight and evenly down each side, a parting extending from nose to end of tail. Very compact and neat, carriage very upright conveying an important air. General outline conveying impression of vigorous and well proportioned body.

Characteristics: Alert, intelligent toy terrier.

Temperament: Spirited with even disposition.

Head and Skull: Rather small and flat, not too prominent or round in skull, nor too long in muzzle; black nose.

Eyes: Medium, dark, sparkling, with sharp intelligent expression and placed to look directly forward. Not prominent. Edge of eyelids dark.

Ears: Small, V-shaped, carried erect, not too far apart, covered with short hair, colour very deep, rich tan.

Mouth: Perfect, regular and complete scissor bite, i.e. upper teeth closely overlapping lower teeth and set square to the jaws. Teeth well placed with even jaws.

Neck: Good reach.

Forequarters: Well laid shoulders, legs straight, well covered with hair of rich golden tan a few shades lighter at ends than at roots, not extending higher on forelegs than elbow.

This is what a champion Yorkshire Terrier looks like when groomed for show.

35

Body: Compact with moderate spring of rib, good loin. Level back.

Hindquarters: Legs quite straight when viewed from behind, moderate turn of stifle. Well covered with hair of rich golden tan a few shades lighter at ends than at roots, not extending higher on hindlegs than stifles.

Feet: Round; nails black.

Tail: Customarily docked to medium length with plenty of hair, darker blue in colour than rest of body, especially at the end of tail. Carried a little higher than level of back.

Gait/Movement: Free with drive; straight action front and behind, retaining level topline.

Coat: Hair on body moderately long, perfectly straight (not wavy), glossy, fine silky texture, not woolly. Fall on head long, rich golden tan, deeper in colour at sides of head, about ear roots and on muzzle where it should be very long. Tan on head not to extend on to neck, nor must any sooty or dark hair intermingle with any of tan.

Colour: Dark steel blue (not silver blue), extending from occiput to root of tail, never mingled with fawn, bronze or dark hairs. Hair on chest rich, bright tan. All tan hair darker at the roots than in middle, shading to still lighter at tips.

With a moustache touching the ground, this magnificent specimen has the silken hair of rich golden tan on the fall of the head.

The young Yorkshire Terrier puppy, a bit scraggly and awkward, hardly resembles its well coiffed mother.

Size: Weight up to 3.1 kgs (7lbs).

Faults: Any departure from the foregoing points should be considered a fault and the seriousness with which the fault should be regarded should be in exact proportion to its degree.

Note: Male animals should have two apparently normal testicles fully descended into the scrotum.

DID YOU KNOW?

The behaviour and personality of your dog will reflect your care and training more than any breed characteristics or indications. Remember that these dogs require a purposeful existence and plan your relationship around activities that serve this most basic and important need. All the good potential of the breed will necessarily follow.

(opposite page) This lovely American champion clearly shows the striking difference between the dark steel blue on the rear portion of the dog and the golden tan hairs hanging from the head.

Scanning electro micrograph of normal and damaged Yorkshire Terrier hairs. Inset depicts split end in hair.

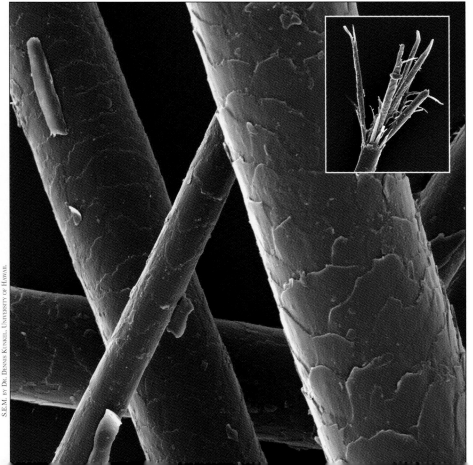

S.E.M. BY DR. DENNIS KUNKEL, UNIVERSITY OF HAWAII.

The body is long coated, with hair hanging straight and evenly down each side.

The head is characterised by small, V-shaped ears, erect and covered with hair.

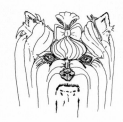

The ears must not be too far apart or held incorrectly, thus spoiling the desired expression.

The muzzle must never be too long; the nose is black.

The mouth must exhibit a perfect scissors bite, with teeth well placed with even jaws.

Your Yorkshire Terrier Puppy

OWNER CONSIDERATIONS

Owning a Yorkshire Terrier is a giant commitment. Accepting the responsibility of dog ownership, even a dog as small and unimposing as a Yorkshire Terrier, must be taken seriously. The dog must be considered in every aspect of the owner's lifestyle. Dogs require attention, not to mention food, water, walks, veterinary care, and lots more. Even though a Yorkshire Terrier will not require as much outside time as a Golden Retriever, for example, it will enjoy a daily walk plus frequent breaks to be in the garden to relieve itself. Long

Acquiring any living pet requires a commitment on your part. This is especially true of a Yorkshire Terrier, who will rely upon you for its every moment.

SPOILING THE YORKIE

Since we know that Yorkies can easily be spoiled, it is wise to advise owners about the dangers of 'spoiling your Yorkie's appetite.' The caloric requirements of a toy dog is about 500 calories per day, so it only takes about two or three treats to throw your Yorkie off his eating schedule. A Yorkie cannot be expected to eat his full day's ration if he has already consumed 300 calories in treats. Spare the cookies and save them for special occasions and training sessions.

weekends and holidays must be planned with the dog in mind. Although the Yorkshire Terrier may be a bit smaller than the family cat, it requires much more commitment than a cat, who is mostly content to look after itself.

The Yorkshire Terrier thrives on the time spent with its special

It is not too difficult to imagine that owning two Yorkies is at least twice the pleasure of owning one. After all, just watching the puppies play with each other is a pleasure you'll miss if you only have one Yorkie.

DID YOU KNOW?

If you lead an erratic, unpredictable life, with daily or weekly changes in your work requirements, consider the problems of owning a puppy. The new puppy has to be fed regularly, socialised (loved, petted, handled, introduced to other people) and, most importantly, allowed to visit outdoors for toilet training. As the dog gets older, it can be more tolerant of deviations in its feeding and toilet relief.

show dog or just a home companion, there are a number of considerations to keep in mind when acquiring a Yorkie.

ACQUIRING A PUPPY

Potential owners should set out to purchase the best Yorkshire Terrier that they can possibly afford. The safest method of obtaining your puppy is to seek out a local reputable breeder. This is suggested

DID YOU KNOW?

Two important documents you will get from the breeder are the pup's pedigree and registration papers. The breeder should register the litter and each pup with The Kennel Club, and it is necessary for you to have the paperwork if you plan on showing or breeding in the future.

Make sure you know the breeder's intentions on which type of registration he will obtain for the pup. There are limited registrations which may prohibit the dog from being shown or from competing in non-conformation trials such as Working or Agility if the breeder feels that the pup is not of sufficient quality to do so. There is also a type of registration that will permit the dog in non-conformation competition only.

If your dog is registered with a Kennel-Club-recognised breed club, then you can register the pup with The Kennel Club yourself. Your breeder can assist you with the specifics of the registration process.

people. There is no breed that depends on its human family as much as a Yorkshire Terrier. Committing yourself to the care of such a giving, loving animal is akin to accepting the responsibility of a child. Although the Yorkie will not grow up and move out of your home when he is seventeen, he will look up to you as a parent and depend on you for food, shelter and affection.

Most Yorkshire Terrier enthusiasts keep the breed as a home companion and not as a show dog. Although the Yorkshire Terrier excels in the show ring, thriving on the attention and the pageantry, most Yorkies never have the opportunity to strut their glamorous selves for the judges and the crowd. Whether you are seeking a even if you are not looking for a show specimen. The novice breeders and pet owners who advertise at attractive prices in the local newspapers are probably kind enough towards their dogs, but perhaps do not have the expertise or facilities required to successfully raise these animals. These pet puppies are frequently badly weaned and left with the mother too long without any supplemental feeding. This lack of proper feeding can cause indiges-

Unless you want to enter dog shows, you don't need a show dog. Get a pet-quality Yorkshire Terrier from a reputable breeder.

tion, rickets, weak bones, poor teeth and other problems. Veterinary bills may soon distort initial savings into financial, or worse, emotional loss.

DID YOU KNOW?

Another important consideration remains to be discussed and that is the sex of your puppy. For a family companion, a Yorkie bitch is the best choice, considering the female's inbred concern for all young creatures and her accompanying tolerance and patience. If you do not intend to spay your pet when she has matured or is well over her growing period, then extra care is required during the times of her heat.

Inquire about inoculations and when the puppy was last dosed for worms. Check the ears. Although many puppies do not have erect ears until five or six months, some movement forward and signs of lifting when the puppy is alerted are good predictors of normal development.

Approach the dam and her puppies. The dam should be friendly and trusting. The puppies should be outgoing and interested in meeting you. Do not be concerned if the litter is limited to two or three pups. Yorkies have very small litters, and a single puppy is not uncommon. The breeder may not be able to give you 'pick of the litter,' since the number of puppies is so limited. Additionally, do not be taken aback if the breeder whom you select tells you that there is six

months to two years' waiting period for a puppy. Since Yorkshires have such small litters and the demand for the breed is high, breeders commonly cannot meet the demand. There is especially true with breeders with established reputations. Perhaps your chosen breeder can recommend another breeder who has

puppies available sooner. If not, you may have to wait for the puppy of your choice.

COMMITMENT OF OWNERSHIP
After considering all of these factors, you have most likely already made some very important decisions about selecting your puppy. You have chosen a Yorkshire Terrier, which means that you have decided which characteristics you

DID YOU KNOW?
You should not even think about buying a puppy that looks sick, undernourished, overly frightened or nervous. Sometimes a timid puppy will warm up to you after a 30-minute 'let's-get-acquainted' session.

A Yorkie dam with five of her puppies. This is an unusually large litter for a Yorkshire Terrier, as litters of one or two are far more common.

Yorkie puppies's ears become erect in time. Breeders explain that the teething period often interferes with the ears, which will re-stand after the phase is over.

Yorkshire Terriers are lovers from the beginning. They quickly bond to their human friends. This warmth is one of the reasons for their huge popularity.

> ### DID YOU KNOW?
>
> Unfortunately, when a puppy is purchased by someone who does not take into consideration the time and attention that dog ownership requires, it is the puppy who suffers when he is either abandoned or placed in a shelter by a frustrated owner. So all of the 'homework' you do in preparation for your pup's arrival will benefit you both. The more informed you are, the more you will know what to expect and the better equipped you will be to handle the ups and downs of raising a puppy. Hopefully, everyone in the household is willing to do his part in raising and caring for the pup. The anticipation of owning a dog often brings a lot of promises from excited family members: 'I will walk him every day,' 'I will feed him,' 'I will housebreak him,' etc., but these things take time and effort, and promises can easily be forgotten once the novelty of the new pet has worn off.

Kissing your Yorkshire Terrier, or any dog, on the mouth is quite unsanitary.

and found a responsible, conscientious person who breeds quality Yorkshire Terriers and who should be a reliable source of help as you and your puppy adjust to life together. If you have observed a litter in action, you have obtained a firsthand look at the dynamics of a puppy 'pack' and, thus, you have gotten to learn about each pup's individual personality—perhaps you have even found one that particularly appeals to you.

However, even if you have not yet found the Yorkshire Terrier puppy of your dreams, observing pups will help you learn to recognise certain behaviour and to determine what a pup's behaviour indicates about his temperament. You will be able to pick out which pups are the leaders, which ones

want in a dog and what type of dog will best fit into your family and lifestyle. If you have selected a breeder, you have gone a step further—you have done your research

comes to deciding on the type of dog you want and finding out about your prospective pup's background. Buying a puppy is not—or should not be—just another whimsical purchase. In fact, this is one instance in which you actually do get to choose your own family! But, you may be thinking, buying a puppy should be fun—it should not be so serious and so much work. If you keep in mind the thought that your puppy is not a cuddly stuffed toy or decorative lawn ornament, but instead will become a real member of your family, you will realise that while buying a puppy

Observe as many Yorkie pups as possible so you can judge what is normal behaviour, how a healthy puppy reacts to you and other stimuli, and how it feels when you handle it.

are less outgoing, which ones are confident, which ones are shy, playful, friendly, aggressive, etc. Equally as important, you will learn to recognise what a healthy pup should look and act like. All of these things will help you in your search, and when you find the Yorkshire Terrier that was meant for you, you will know it!

Researching your breed, selecting a responsible breeder and observing as many pups as possible are all important steps on the way to dog ownership. It may seem like a lot of effort…and you have not even brought the pup home yet! Remember, though, you cannot be too careful when it

DID YOU KNOW?

Many good breeders will offer you insurance with your new puppy, which is an excellent idea. The first few weeks of insurance will probably be covered free of charge or with only minimal cost, allowing you to take up the policy when this expires. If you own a pet dog, it is sensible to take out such a policy as veterinary fees can be high, although routine vaccinations and boosters are not covered. Look carefully at the many options open to you before deciding which suits best.

A veterinary surgeon should have examined the parents of your puppy before they were bred to ascertain whether any inherited eye abnormalities could be passed to their puppies.

of this? Well, you should not worry about it; in fact, you will probably find that once your Yorkshire Terrier pup gets used to his new home, he will fall into his place in the family quite naturally. But it never hurts to emphasise the commitment of dog ownership. With some time and patience, it is really not too difficult to raise a curious and exuberant Yorkshire Terrier pup to be a well-adjusted and well-mannered adult dog—a dog that could be your most loyal friend.

PREPARING PUPPY'S PLACE IN YOUR HOME

Researching your breed and finding a breeder are only two aspects of the 'homework' you will have to do before bringing

is a pleasurable and exciting endeavour, it is not something to be taken lightly. Relax…the fun will start when the pup comes home!

Always keep in mind that a puppy is nothing more than a baby in a furry disguise…a baby who is virtually helpless in a human world and who trusts his owner for fulfilment of his basic needs for survival. That goes beyond food, water and shelter; your pup needs care, protection, guidance and love. If you are not prepared to commit to this, then you are not prepared to own a dog.

Wait a minute, you say. How hard could this be? All of my neighbours own dogs and they seem to be doing just fine. Why should I have to worry about all

DID YOU KNOW?
Your selection of a good puppy can be determined by your needs. A show potential or a good pet? It is your choice. Every puppy, however, should be of good temperament. Although show-quality puppies are bred and raised with emphasis on physical conformation, responsible breeders strive for equally good temperament. Do not buy from a breeder who concentrates solely on physical beauty at the expense of personality.

your Yorkshire Terrier puppy home. You will also have to prepare your home and family for the new addition. Much like you would prepare a nursery for a newborn baby, you will need to designate a place in your home that will be the puppy's own. How you prepare your home will depend on how much freedom the dog will be allowed: will he be confined to one room or a specific area in the house, or will he be allowed to roam as he pleases? Whatever you decide, you must ensure that he has a place that he can 'call his own.'

When you bring your new puppy into your home, you are bringing him into what will become his home as well. Obviously, you did not buy a puppy so that he could take over your house, but in order for a puppy to grow into a stable, well-adjusted dog, he has to feel comfortable in his surroundings. Remember, he is leaving the warmth and security of his mother and littermates, plus the familiarity of the only place he has ever known, so it is important to make

DID YOU KNOW?
Breeders rarely release puppies until they are at least eight weeks of age. This is an acceptable age for most breeds of dog, excepting toy breeds which are not released until around 12 weeks, given their petite sizes. If a breeder has a puppy that is 12 weeks or more, it is likely well socialised and housetrained. Be sure that it is otherwise healthy before deciding to take it home.

his transition as easy as possible. By preparing a place in your home for the puppy, you are making him feel as welcome as possible in a strange new place. It should not take him long to get used to it, but the sudden shock of being transplanted is somewhat trau-

Your Yorkie puppy will enjoy the grass, especially when it is comfortably warm, but keep in mind that fleas, ticks and other parasitic organisms can lurk in the grass.

DID YOU KNOW?
A good breeder should not be afraid to give you a health guarantee as well as a guarantee that the puppy will pass a temperament test administered by a vet or trained dog behaviourist.

Breeders train their puppies never to defecate or eliminate in their clean sleeping areas. Crate training continues this philosophy and requires owners to use a crate once the Yorkie pup arrives home.

Crates come in all shapes, sizes and materials. A simple wire crate with a blanket or cushion is satisfactory for carrying the Yorkie outside the home. As a refuge, the crate has to open so the dog can easily go in and out.

matic for a young pup. Imagine how a small child would feel in the same situation—that is how your puppy must be feeling. It is up to you to reassure him and to let him know, 'Little fellow, you are going to like it here!'

WHAT YOU SHOULD BUY
CRATE

To someone unfamiliar with the use of crates in dog training, it may seem like punishment to shut a dog in a crate; this is not the case at all. Crates are not cruel—crates have many humane and highly effective uses in dog care and training. For example, crate training is a very popular and very successful housebreak-

ing method; a crate can keep your dog safe during travel; and, perhaps most importantly, a crate provides your dog with a place of his own in your home. It serves as a 'doggie bedroom' of sorts—your Yorkshire Terrier can curl up in his crate when he wants to sleep or when he just needs a break. Many dogs sleep in their crates overnight. When lined with soft blankets and filled with his favourite toys, a crate becomes a cosy pseudo-den

for your dog. Like his ancestors, he too will seek out the comfort and retreat of a den—you just happen to be providing him with something a little more luxurious than leaves and twigs lining a dirty ditch.

As far as purchasing a crate, the type that you buy is up to you. It will most likely be one of

DID YOU KNOW?
If the breeder from whom you are buying a puppy asks you a lot of personal questions, do not be insulted. Such a breeder wants to be sure that you will be a fit provider for his puppy.

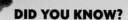

the two most popular types: wire or fibreglass. There are advantages and disadvantages to each type. For example, a wire crate is more open, allowing the air to flow through and affording the dog a view of what is going on around him. A fibreglass crate, however, is sturdier and can double as a travel crate since it provides more protection for the dog. Purchase the smallest crate available from the pet shop. This crate will suit the Yorkie in puppyhood and adulthood—a real advantage to choosing the smallest breed known to man!

BEDDING

A blanket or two in the dog's crate will help the dog feel more at home. First, the blankets will take the place of the leaves, twigs, etc., that the pup would use in the wild to make a den; the pup can make his own 'burrow' in the crate. Although your pup is far removed from his den-making ancestors, the denning instinct is still a part of his genetic makeup. Second, until you bring your pup home,

he has been sleeping amidst the warmth of his mother and littermates, and while a blanket is not the same as a warm, breathing body, it still provides heat and something with which to snuggle. You will want to wash your pup's blankets frequently in case he has an accident in his crate, and replace or remove any blanket that becomes ragged and starts to fall apart.

PHOTO COURTESY OF MIKKI PET PRODUCTS.

Your local pet shop will have many crates of different sizes and shapes. Discuss your needs (carrying crate, car crate, housebreaking and training crate, etc.) with your local pet shop operator.

51

Toys

Toys are a must for dogs of all ages, especially for curious playful pups. Puppies are the 'children' of the dog world, and what child does not love toys? Chew toys provide enjoyment to both dog and owner—your dog will enjoy playing with his favourite toys, while you will enjoy the fact that they distract him from your expensive shoes and leather sofa. Puppies love to chew; in fact, chewing is a physical need for pups as they are

DID YOU KNOW?

During crate training, you should partition off the section of the crate in which the pup stays. If he is given too big an area, this will hinder your training efforts. Crate training is based on the fact that a dog does not like to soil his sleeping quarters, so it is ineffective to keep a pup in a crate that is so big that he can eliminate in one end and get far enough away from it to sleep. Also, you want to make the crate den-like for the pup. Blankets and a favourite toy will make the crate cosy for the small Yorkie; as he grows, you may want to evict some of his 'roommates' to make more room.

It will take some coaxing at first, but be patient. Given some time to get used to it, your pup will adapt to his new home-within-a-home quite nicely.

DID YOU KNOW?

With a big variety of dog toys available, and so many that look like they would be a lot of fun for a dog, be careful in your selection. It is amazing what a set of puppy teeth can do to an innocent-looking toy, so, obviously, safety is a major consideration. Be sure to choose the most durable products that you can find. Hard nylon bones and toys are a safe bet, and many of them are offered in different scents and flavours that will be sure to capture your Yoekie's attention. It is always fun to play a game of catch with your dog, and there are balls and flying discs that are specially made to withstand dog teeth.

teething, and everything looks appetising! The full range of your possessions—from old dishrag to Oriental rug—are fair game in the eyes of a teething pup. Puppies are not all that discerning when it comes to finding something to literally 'sink their teeth into'—everything tastes great!

Stuffed toys are another option; these are good to put in the dog's crate to give him some company. Be careful of these, as a pup can de-stuff one pretty quickly, and stay away from stuffed toys with small plastic

PHOTO COURTESY OF MIKKI PET PRODUCTS.

Your local pet shop will have a large assortment of toys suitable for your Yorkie. Do not buy children's toys for dogs as they may be toxic or easily torn.

eyes or parts that a pup could choke on. Similarly, squeaky toys are quite popular. There are dogs that will come running from anywhere in the house at the first sound from their

favourite squeaky friend. Again, if a pup de-stuffs one of these, the small plastic squeaker inside can be dangerous if swallowed. Monitor the condition of your pup's toys carefully and get rid of any that have been chewed to the point of becoming potentially dangerous.

Be careful of natural bones, which have a tendency to splinter into sharp, dangerous pieces. Also be careful of rawhide, which after enough chewing can turn into pieces that are easy to swallow, and also watch out for the mushy mess it can turn into on your carpet.

Yorkies like to play and can keep themselves occupied for hours if provided with interesting toys and bones.

53

Your local pet shop will have a large variety of leads in different colours and made from different materials.

PHOTO COURTESY OF MIKKI PET PRODUCTS.

LEAD

A nylon lead is probably the best option as it is the most resistant to puppy teeth should your pup take a liking to chewing on his lead. Of course, this is a habit that should be nipped in the bud, but if your pup likes to chew on his lead he has a very slim chance of being able to chew through the strong nylon. Nylon leads are also light-weight, which is good for a young Yorkshire Terrier who is just get-ting used to the idea of walking on a lead. For everyday walking and safety purposes, the nylon lead is a good choice. As your pup grows up and gets used to walking on the lead, and can do it politely, you may want to purchase a flexible lead, which allows you either to extend the length to give the dog a broader area to explore or to pull in the lead when you want to keep him close.

COLLAR

Your pup should get used to wear-ing a collar all the time since you will want to attach his ID tags to his collar. Also, the lead and collar go hand in hand—you have to attach the lead to something! A lightweight nylon collar will be a good choice; make sure that it fits snugly enough so that the pup can-not wriggle out of it, but loose enough so that it will not be uncomfortably tight around the pup's neck. You should be able to fit a finger in between the pup and the collar. It may take some time for your pup to get used to wearing the collar, but soon he will not even notice that it is there.

FOOD AND WATER BOWLS

Your pup will need two bowls, one for food and one for water. You may want two sets of bowls, one for inside and one for outside, depending on where the dog will be fed and where he will be spend-ing most of his time. Stainless steel or sturdy plastic bowls are popular choices. Although plastic bowls are more chewable, dogs tend not to chew on the steel variety, which can also be sterilised.

CLEANING SUPPLIES

A pup that is not housetrained means you will be doing a lot of cleaning until he is. Accidents will occur, which is okay for now because he does not know any better. All you can do is clean up any 'accidents'—old rags, towels, newspapers and a safe disinfectant are good to have on hand. Be sure that you thoroughly remove the odour from any mishaps. Dogs tend to repeat offences when they can detect a familiar scent.

BEYOND THE BASICS

The items previously discussed are the bare necessities. You will find out what else you need as you go along—grooming supplies, flea/tick protection, baby gates to partition a room, etc.—these things will vary depending on your situation. It is just important that right away you have everything you need to feed and make your Yorkshire Terrier comfortable in his first few days at home.

PUPPY-PROOFING YOUR HOME

Aside from making sure that your Yorkshire Terrier will be comfortable in your home, you also have to make sure that your home is safe for your Yorkshire Terrier. This means taking precautions to make sure that your pup will not get into anything he should not get into and that there is nothing within his reach that may harm him should he sniff it, chew it, inspect it, etc. This probably seems obvious since, while you are primarily concerned with your pup's safety,

The toughest night with your Yorkie puppy will be the first night, for both the puppy and the family.

at the same time you do not want your belongings to be ruined. Breakables should be placed out of reach if your dog is to have full run of the house. If he is to be limited to certain places within the house, keep any potentially dangerous items in the 'off-limits' areas. An electrical cord can pose a danger should the puppy decide to taste it—and who is going to convince a pup that it would not make a great chew toy? Cords should be fastened tightly against the wall. If your dog is going to spend time in a crate, make sure that there is nothing near his crate that he can reach if he sticks his

Puppies should have food and water available at all times. As your Yorkie gets older his need for frequent feedings will diminish. Adult Yorkies usually require one or two meals per day.

curious little nose or paws through the openings. And just as you would with a child, keep all household cleaners and chemicals where the pup cannot get to them.

It is just as important to make sure that the outside of your home is safe. Of course your puppy should never be unsupervised, but a pup let loose in the garden will want to run and explore, and he should be granted that freedom. Do not let a fence give you a false sense of security; you would be surprised how crafty (and persistent) a dog can be in figuring out how to dig under and squeeze his way through small holes, or to climb over a fence. Be sure to repair or secure any gaps in the fence. Check the fence periodically to ensure that it is in good shape and make repairs as needed; a very determined pup may return to the same spot to 'work on it' until he is able to get through.

'You can't teach an old dog new tricks' is an untrue expression, but it is easier to train a pup.

FIRST TRIP TO THE VET

Okay, you have picked out your puppy, your home and family are ready, now all you have to do is pick your Yorkshire Terrier up from the breeder and the fun begins, right? Well…not so fast. Something else you need to pre-

pare for is your pup's first trip to the veterinary surgeon. Perhaps the breeder can recommend someone in the area that specialises in Yorkshire Terriers, or maybe you know some other Yorkshire Terrier owners who can suggest a good vet. Either way, you should have an appointment arranged for your pup before you pick him up; plan on taking him for a checkup within the first few days of bringing him home.

The pup's first visit will consist of an overall examination to make sure that the pup does not have any problems that are not apparent to the eye. The veterinary surgeon will also set up a schedule for the pup's vaccinations; the breeder will inform you of which ones the pup has already received and the vet can continue from there.

last thing you want to do is smother him, as this will only frighten him further. This is not to say that human contact is not extremely necessary at this stage, because this is the time

INTRODUCTION TO THE FAMILY

Everyone in the house will be excited about the puppy coming home and will want to pet him and play with him, but it is best to make the introduction low-key so as not to overwhelm the puppy. He is apprehensive already; it is the first time he has been separated from his mother and the breeder, and the ride to your home is likely the first time he has been in an auto. The

DID YOU KNOW?
Taking your dog from the breeder to your home in a car, can be a very uncomfortable experience for both of you. The puppy will have been taken from his warm, friendly, safe environment and brought into a strange new environment. An environment that moves. Be prepared for loose bowels, urination, crying, whining and even fear biting. With proper love and encouragement when you arrive home, the stress of the trip should quickly disappear.

when an instant connection between the pup and his human family are formed. Gentle petting and soothing words should help console him, as well as just putting him down and letting him explore on his own (under your watchful eye, of course).

The pup may approach the family members or may busy himself with exploring for awhile. Gradually, each person should spend some time with the pup, one at a time, crouching down to get as close to the pup's level as possible and letting him sniff their

DID YOU KNOW?

Use treats to bribe your dog into a desired behaviour. Try small pieces of hard cheese or freeze-dried liver. Never offer chocolate as it has toxic qualities for dogs.

hands and petting him gently. He definitely needs human attention and he needs to be touched—this is how to form an immediate bond. Just remember that the pup is experiencing a lot of things for the first time, all at the same time. There are new people, new noises, new smells, and new things to investigate, so be gentle, be affectionate and be as comforting as you can be.

Don't overwhelm your new Yorkshire Terrier during his first days in your home. He has his whole life to explore and experience the world around him.

YOUR PUP'S FIRST NIGHT HOME
You have travelled home with your new charge safely in his basket or crate. He's been to the vet for a thorough check-over; he has been weighed, his papers examined; per-

haps he has even been vaccinated and wormed as well. He has met the family, licked the whole family, including the excited children and the less-than-happy cat. He has explored his area, his new bed, the garden and anywhere else he has been permitted. He has eaten his first meal at home and relieved himself in the proper place. He has heard lots of new sounds, smelled new friends and seen more of the outside world than ever before.

DID YOU KNOW?

It will take at least two weeks for your puppy to become accustomed to his new surroundings. Give him lots of love, attention, handling, frequent opportunity to relieve himself, a diet he likes to eat and a place he can call his own.

That was the just the first day! He is worn out and is ready for bed...or so you think!

It is puppy's first night and you are ready to say 'Good night'—keep in mind that this is puppy's first night ever to be sleeping alone. His dam and littermates are no longer at paw's length away and he is a bit scared, cold and lonely. Be reassuring to your new family member. This is not the time to spoil him and give in to his inevitable whining.

Puppies whine. They whine to let the others know where they are and hopefully to get company out of it. Place your pup in his new bed or crate in his room and close the door. Mercifully, he will fall asleep without a peep. If the inevitable occurs, ignore the whining; he is fine. Be strong and keep his interest in mind. Do not allow your heart to become guilty and visit the pup. He will fall asleep.

Many breeders recommend placing a piece of bedding from his former homestead in his new bed so that he recognises the scent of his littermates. Others still advise placing a hot water bottle in his bed for warmth. This latter may be a good idea provided the pup does not attempt to suckle—he will get good and wet and may not fall asleep so fast.

Puppy's first night can be somewhat stressful for the pup and his new family. Remember that you are setting the tone of nighttime at your house. Unless you want to play with your pup every evening at 10 p.m., midnight and 2 a.m., do not initiate the habit. Surely your family will thank you, and so will your pup!

He doesn't know it yet, but tonight he'll be sleeping alone for the first time in his life. He is certainly not prepared for a lonely night without his mum....are you?

Don't play too roughly with your Yorkie. Keep in mind that, despite your Yorkie's big-dog confidence, he's still a petite fellow that must be handled with care.

PREVENTING PUPPY PROBLEMS
SOCIALISATION

Now that you have done all of the preparatory work and have helped your pup get accustomed to his new home and family, it is about time for you to have some fun! Socialising your Yorkshire Terrier pup gives you the opportunity to

sure to other animals. Be careful during the eight-to-ten-week period, also known as the fear period. The interaction he receives during this time should be gentle and reassuring.

Once your pup has received his necessary vaccinations, feel free to take him out and about (on his lead, of course). Take him around the neighbourhood, take him on your daily errands, let people pet him, let him meet other dogs and pets, etc. Puppies do not have to try to make friends; there will be no shortage of people who will want to introduce themselves. Just make sure that you carefully supervise each

show off your new friend, and your pup gets to reap the benefits of being an adorable furry creature that people will fuss over, want to pet and, in general, think is absolutely precious!

Besides getting to know his new family, your puppy should be exposed to other people, animals and situations. This will help him become well adjusted as he grows up and less prone to being timid or fearful of the new things he will encounter. Your pup's socialisation began at the breeder's, now it is your responsibility to continue. The socialisation he receives up until the age of 12 weeks is the most critical, as this is the time when he forms his impressions of the outside world. Lack of socialisation can manifest itself in fear and aggression as the dog grows up. He needs lots of human contact, affection, handling and expo-

Having a parrot sit on your Yorkie puppy's head would qualify as a 'new experience' for your dog. Keep socialisation in perspective—don't overwhelm your pup with too much activity.

meeting. If the neighbourhood children want to say hello, for example, that is great—children and pups most often make great companions. But sometimes an excited child can unintentionally handle a pup too roughly, or an overzealous pup can playfully nip a little too hard. You want to make socialisation experiences positive ones; what a pup learns during this very formative stage will impact his attitude toward future encounters. A pup that has a bad experience with a child may grow up to be a dog that is shy around or aggressive toward children, and you want your dog to be comfortable around everyone.

CONSISTENCY IN TRAINING
Dogs, being pack animals, natural-

> **DID YOU KNOW?**
> Chewing goes hand in hand with nipping in the sense that a teething puppy is always looking for a way to soothe his aching gums. In this case, instead of chewing on you, he may have taken a liking to your favourite shoe or something else which he should not be chewing. Again, realise that this is a normal canine behaviour that does not need to be discouraged, only redirected. Your pup just needs to be taught what is acceptable to chew on and what is off limits. Consistently tell him NO when you catch him chewing on something forbidden and give him a chew toy. Conversely, praise him when you catch him chewing on something appropriate. In this way you are discouraging the inappropriate behaviour and reinforcing the desired behaviour. The puppy chewing should stop after his adult teeth have come in, but most adult dogs continue to chew for various reasons—perhaps because he is bored, perhaps to relieve tension, or perhaps he just likes to chew. That is why it is important to redirect his chewing when he is still young.

Hello there! New canine introductions should not be made without both dogs' being restrained on a leash. Some dogs are naturally friendly and others are unexpectedly aggressive. Caution is always advised.

ly need a leader, or else they try to establish dominance in their packs. When you bring a dog into your family, who becomes the leader and who becomes the 'pack' are entirely up to you! Your pup's intuitive quest for dominance, coupled with the fact that it is nearly impossible to look at an adorable Yorkshire Terrier pup, with his 'puppy-dog' eyes and not cave in, give the pup almost an unfair advantage in getting the upper hand! And a pup will definitely test the waters to see what he can and cannot get away with. Do not

DID YOU KNOW?

Young dogs with a timid personality and temperament are much easier to train than more assertive dogs. If you have a puppy that seems untrainable, take him to a trainer or behaviourist. The dog may have a personality problem that requires the help of a professional, or perhaps you need help in learning how to train your dog.

courage bad behaviour in a young developing pup than to wait until the pup's bad behaviour becomes the adult dog's bad habit. There are some problems that are especially prevalent in puppies as they develop.

NIPPING

As puppies start to teethe, they feel the need to sink their teeth into anything…unfortunately that includes your fingers, arms, hair, toes…whatever happens to be available. You may find this behaviour cute for about the first five seconds…until you feel just how sharp those puppy teeth are. This is something you want to discourage immediately and consistently

give in to those pleading eyes—stand your ground when it comes to disciplining the pup and make sure that all family members do the same. It will only confuse the pup when Mother tells him to get off the couch when he is used to sitting up there with Father to watch the nightly news. Avoid discrepancies by having all members of the household decide on the rules before the pup even comes home…and be consistent in enforcing them! Early training shapes the dog's personality, so you cannot be unclear in what you expect.

Even if your Yorkie cries, whines and begs, don't feed him from the table or you will have a beggar for life. Besides, human food can spoil your Yorkie's balanced diet.

COMMON PUPPY PROBLEMS

The best way to prevent problems is to be proactive in stopping an undesirable behaviour as soon as it starts. The old saying 'You can't teach an old dog new tricks' does not necessarily hold true, but it is true that it is much easier to dis-

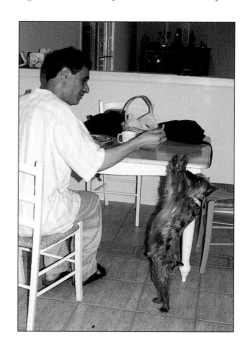

with a firm 'No!' (or whatever number of firm 'No's' it takes for him to understand that you mean business) and replace your finger with an appropriate chew toy. While this behaviour is merely annoying when the dog is still young, it can become dangerous as your Yorkshire Terrier's adult teeth grow in and his jaws develop, if he thinks that it is okay to gnaw on human appendages.

CRYING/WHINING

Your pup will often cry, whine, whimper, howl or make some type of commotion when he is left alone. This is basically his way of calling out for attention, of calling out to make sure that you know he is there and that you have not forgotten about him. He feels insecure when he is left alone, for example, when you are out of the house and he is in his crate or when you are in another part of the house and he cannot see you. The noise he is making is an expression of the anxiety he feels at being alone, so he needs to be taught that being alone is okay. You are not actually training the dog to stop making noise, you are training him to feel comfortable when he is alone and thus removing the need for him to make the noise. This is where the crate filled with cosy blankets and toys comes in handy. You want to know that he is safe when you are not there to supervise, and you know that he will be safe in his crate rather than roaming freely about the house. In order for the pup to stay in his crate without making a fuss, he needs to be comfortable in his crate. On that note, it is extremely important that the crate is never used as a form of punishment, or the pup will have a negative association with the crate.

Accustom the pup to the crate in short, gradually increasing time intervals in which you put him in the crate, maybe with a treat, and stay in the room with him. If he cries or makes a fuss, do not go to him, but stay in his sight. Gradually he will realise that staying in his crate is all right without your help, and it will not be so traumatic for him when you are not around. You may want to leave the radio on softly when you leave the house; the sound of human voices may be comforting to him.

DID YOU KNOW?
The majority of problems that are commonly seen in young pups will disappear as your Yorkie gets older. However, how you deal with problems when he is young will determine how he reacts to discipline as an adult dog. It is important to establish who is boss (hopefully it will be you!) right away when you are first bonding with your Yorkie. This bond will set the tone for the rest of your life together.

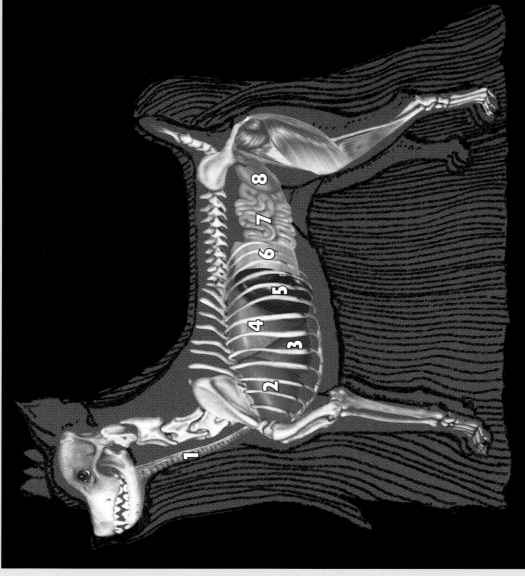

Internal Organs with Skeletal Structure

1. Oesophagus
2. Lungs
3. Gall Bladder
4. Liver
5. Kidney
6. Stomach
7. Intestines
8. Urinary Bladder

Everyday Care of Your Yorkshire Terrier

DIETARY AND FEEDING CONSIDERATIONS

You have probably heard it a thousand times, you are what you eat. Believe it or not, it is very true. For dogs, they are what you feed them because they have little choice in the matter. Even those people who truly want to feed their dogs the best often cannot do so because they do not know which foods are best for their dog.

Dog foods are produced in three basic types: dry, semi-moist and canned or tinned. Dry foods are for the cost conscious because they are much less expensive than semi-moist and canned. Dry foods contain the least fat and the most preservatives. Most tinned foods are 60–70-percent water, while semi-moist foods are so full of sugar that they are the least preferred by owners, though dogs welcome them (as does a child sweets).

Three stages of development must be considered when selecting a diet for your dog: the puppy stage, the mid-age or adult stage and the senior age or geriatric stage.

The diet for your new Yorkie puppy must come from a recommendation from the breeder and/or your vet. The idea is not to change the puppy's diet too radically too fast.

PUPPY STAGE

Puppies have a natural instinct to suck milk from their mother's breasts. They should exhibit this behaviour the first day of their lives. If they do not suckle within

a few hours you should attempt to put them onto their mother's nipple. Their failure to feed means you have to feed them yourself under the advice and guidance of a veterinary surgeon. This will involve a baby bottle and a special formula. Their mother's milk is much better than any formula because it contains colostrum, a sort of antibiotic milk which protects the puppy during the first eight to ten weeks of their lives.

A Yorkie isn't considered an adult until he stops growing.

Puppies should be allowed to nurse for six weeks and they should be slowly weaned away from their mother by introducing small portions of tinned meat after they are about one month old. The first three weeks of the Yorkshire Terrier

puppy's life require extra caution from the breeder as the breed, due to its small size, is susceptible to neonatal hypoglycemia, also called low blood sugar. Hypoglycemia is a concern of most of the small toy breeds and in very young pups the concern is due to the limited reserves of glycogen and the fact that the dog's liver enzymes are not yet functioning fully. For this reason, supplemental feedings are needed. Hypoglycemia can be expressed in shaking, tremors, and nervousness. Discuss the condition with your vet so that you are prepared to treat any incidence in a young pup.

By the time they are eight weeks old, they should be completely weaned and fed solely a puppy dry food. During this weaning period, their diet is most important as the puppy grows fastest during its first year of life. Growth foods can be recommended by your veterinary surgeon and the puppy should be kept on this diet for 9 to 12 months.

Puppy diets should be balanced for your dog's needs and supplements of vitamins, minerals and protein should not be necessary.

ADULT DIETS

A dog is considered an adult when it has stopped growing. The growth is in height and/or length. Do not consider the dog's weight when the decision is

What are you feeding your dog?

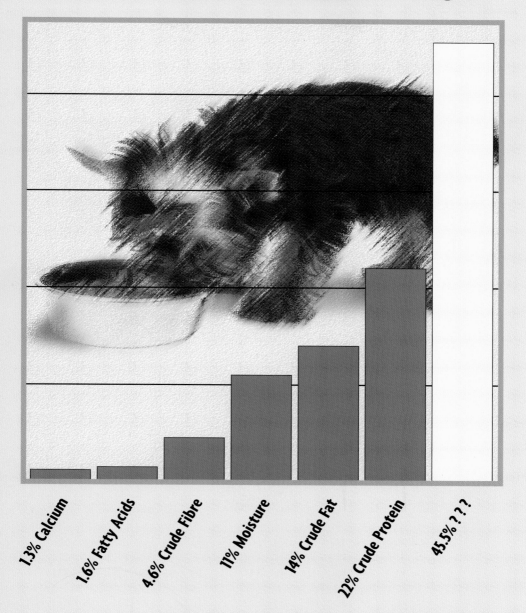

1.3% Calcium | 1.6% Fatty Acids | 4.6% Crude Fibre | 11% Moisture | 14% Crude Fat | 22% Crude Protein | 45.5% ? ? ?

Read the label on your dog food. Most manufacturers merely advise you of 50-55% of the contents, leaving the other 45% in doubt.

There is no single best diet for Yorkies or any other breed for that matter. With a coat breed like the Yorkshire Terrier, a proper balanced diet shines through in every glistening hair.

made to switch from a puppy diet to a maintenance diet. Again you should rely upon your veterinary surgeon to recommend an acceptable maintenance diet. Major dog food manufacturers specialise in this type of food and it is just necessary for you to select the one best suited to your dog's needs. Active dogs may have different requirements than sedate dogs.

A Yorkshire Terrier reaches adulthood at about two years of age, though some dogs mature as late as three years.

DIETS FOR SENIOR DOGS

At around seven or eight years of age, the Yorkshire Terrier can be considered a senior. As dogs get older, their metabolism changes. The older dog usually exercises less, moves more slowly and sleeps more. This change in lifestyle and physiological performance requires a change in diet. Since these changes take place slowly, they might not be recognisable. What is easily recognisable is weight gain. By continually feeding your dog an adult maintenance diet when it is slowing down metabolically, your dog will gain weight. Obesity in an older dog compounds the health problems that already accompany old age.

As your dog gets older, few of their organs function up to par. The kidneys slow down and the intestines become less efficient. These age-related factors are best handled with a change in diet and a change in feeding schedule to give smaller portions that are more easily digested.

There is no single best diet for every older dog. While many dogs do well on light or senior diets, other dogs do better on puppy diets or other special premium diets such as lamb and rice.

Be sensitive to your senior Yorkshire Terrier's diet and this will help control other problems that may arise with your old friend.

WATER

Just as your dog needs proper nutrition from his food, water is an essential "nutrient" as well. Water keeps the dog's body properly hydrated and promotes normal function of the body's systems. During housebreaking it is necessary to keep an eye on how much water your Yorkshire Terrier is drinking, but once he is reliably trained he should have access to clean fresh water at all times. Make sure that the dog's water bowl is clean, and change the water often.

EXERCISE

All dogs require some form of exercise, regardless of the breed. A sedentary lifestyle is as harmful to a dog as it is to a person. Fortunately for the Yorkshire Terrier owner, meeting the breed's requirements is simple. Regular walks, play sessions in the garden, or letting the dog run free

Clean water, preferably without chlorine or fluorine, changed daily, at room temperature, is what is needed for your Yorkie's basic health requirement. Bottled water is the preferred variety for Yorkies.

for the Yorkshire Terrier's coat. Any experienced dog person will agree with the adage, 'First you breed a coat, then you feed a coat.' Combing, brushing and bathing are secondary. Nevertheless, the Yorkshire Terrier is a true 'coat breed,' which means its long, silky hair in its unique blue colouration is one of its hallmarks. Keeping the Yorkie in a full-length coat requires special care, and is usually only pursued by the show set. Pet owners usually keep the Yorkie's coat trimmed to a manageable length. Indeed the dog's fall (tuft of hair on the head) can impede the Yorkie's eating (by dangling into the food bowl), and

Keeping a Yorkshire Terrier in a full-length show coat requires daily commitment of the owner. While having such a glamourous chap around the home is rewarding, it's a decision the owner must make.

in the garden under your supervision are all sufficient forms of exercise for the Yorkshire Terrier. Not only is exercise essential to keep the dog's body fit, it is essential to his mental well-being. A bored dog will find something to do, which often manifests itself in some type of destructive behaviour. In this sense, it is essential for the owner's mental well-being as well!

GROOMING

Whereas the Yorkshire Terrier does not require much special care or accommodation in terms of feeding, exercise or space, the care of the coat does place considerable demand on the owner. Grooming is not the first concern

the characteristic moustache and beard can easily be damaged in chewing and playing. A Yorkie kept in full coat must be supervised when exercising or playing since the coat is easily damaged and tangled. Most owners tie the coat up so that the dog can manoeuvre about more freely and enjoy frolicking about in the garden. Never sacrifice the exercise and sunshine for the sake of a long coat.

Owners of show Yorkies must familiarise themselves with the art of wrapping the Yorkie coat, a very complicated procedure involving over two dozens 'paper wraps.' By wrapping the coat, the coat is protected from breaking off and becoming worn from trailing along the floor. If you are considering keeping the coat at its full length for showing the dog, discuss wrapping with the breeder or some other Yorkie expert. It can not be sufficiently explained in a book and needs to be demonstrated to understand properly.

Accustom the young Yorkie to a daily brushing regimen immediately. There is nothing amusing about wrestling with a Yorkie every morning simply to brush its coat. Most Yorkies welcome the attention, but early acclimation is well advised. For the young puppy, a long bristle brush will help to keep the growing coat tidy. Avoid brushing the puppy's face with the brush since a slight slip of the hand

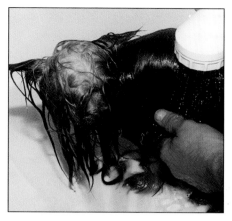

Wash the Yorkie with warm water. Use a very low-pressure spray.

Be careful never to spray directly into your Yorkie's face. Given the delicate nature of the breed's eyes, not to mention keeping the ears dry, spraying should be avoided on the dog's head as much as possible.

Combing through the Yorkie's hair after a bath should be done gently so as not to damage the coat.

Gentle drying with a small machine is preferable to just letting the dog dry in the air. The stream of air should be warm and not too hot so as not to harm the dog.

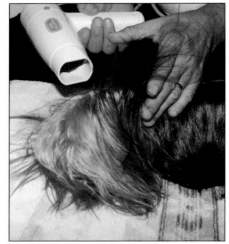

Use a pin brush to assist in the drying process to avoid creating any knots or tangles in the coat.

What price glamour! For a dog as naturally beautiful as the Yorkshire Terrier, doesn't this seem like a lot of effort? It's worth it... we're almost finished.

can badly injure a Yorkie's eyes. Since puppies tend to be busy, an occasional bath may be in order to keep the baby smelling clean and fresh. If the puppy is still eating wet food, the owner will need to wash the dog's face after every meal. Many owners start the Yorkie on dry food simply to keep the dog as clean as possible.

Daily brushing is effective for removing dead hair and stimulating the dog's natural oils to add shine and a healthy look to the coat. For the Yorkie, daily brushing will minimise tangles and mats, get rid of dust and dandruff, and remove any dead hair. On the adult a natural bristle brush used from the skin to the end of the hair, through each layer of hair, is the best course of action. Never skip a day's grooming session or the next day will be more difficult. Over brushing should be avoided since it inevitably causes split ends. The application of oil or lanolin is recommended by most breeders in order to keep the Yorkshire's lustrous coat looking its best. Oil stimulates the hair and prevents the hair from becoming matted.

BATHING

Dogs do not need to be bathed as often as humans, but regular bathing is essential for healthy skin and a healthy, shiny coat. Again, like most anything, if you accustom your pup to being bathed as a puppy, it will be second nature by the time he grows up. You want your dog to be at ease in the bath or else it could end up a wet, soapy, messy ordeal for both of you!

Brush your Yorkshire Terrier thoroughly before wetting his coat. This will get rid of most mats and tangles, which are harder to remove when the coat is wet. Make sure that your dog has a good non-slip surface to stand on. Begin by wetting the dog's

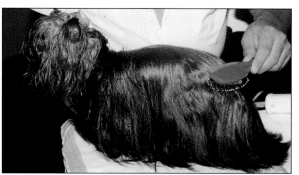

Brushing the damp Yorkie requires a special brush with the ends of the bristles covered with plastic.

Don't forget the top of the head. The topknot is essential to the proper Yorkshire Terrier expression.

DID YOU KNOW?

The use of human soap products like shampoo, bubble bath and soap can be very deleterious to a Yorkie's coat and skin. Human products are too strong and remove the protective oils coating the dog's hair and skin (making him water resistant).

Your Yorkie will need a bath when he gets a dirty coat or when the veterinary surgeon prescribes a medicated bath. In any case, only use shampoo made especially for dogs.

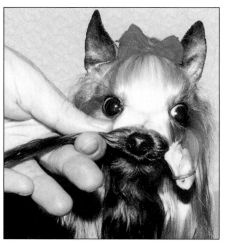

The moustache must be rolled and securely protected with a paper wrapper.

Wrapping the Yorkie coat in paper requires an experienced groomer or handler. Don't expect to read this book and then attempt to groom your new show contender. Seek professional assistance if you are interested in showing your Yorkie.

DID YOU KNOW?

Once you are sure that the dog is thoroughly rinsed, squeeze the excess water out of the coat with your hand and dry him with a heavy towel. You may choose to blow-dry his coat or just let it dry naturally. In cold weather, never allow your dog outside with a wet coat.

There are 'dry bath' products on the market, which are sprays and powders intended for spot cleaning, that can be used between regular baths, if necessary. They are not substitutes for regular baths, but they are easy to use for touch-ups as they do not require rinsing.

coat. A shower or hose attachment is necessary for thoroughly wetting and rinsing the coat. Check the water temperature to make sure that it is neither too hot nor too cold.

Next, apply shampoo to the dog's coat and work it into a good lather. You should purchase a shampoo that is made for dogs; do not use a product made for human hair. Washing the head last; you do not want shampoo to drip into the dog's eyes while you are washing the rest of his body. Work the shampoo all the way down to the skin. You can use this opportunity to check the

Considering the complexity of this grooming routine, would you like to be the 'guinea pig' of an inexperienced beautician?

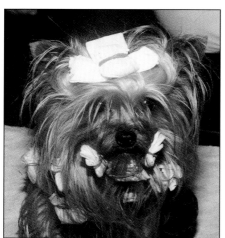

BOWING THE TOPKNOT

The Yorkshire Terrier, like the other long-coated toy breeds, typically sports a topknot on its head. The fall, or the long hair on the head, is gathered and tied with a silky ribbon or bow, contributing to the Yorkshire Terrier's unique expression. When forming a topknot, gather all the hair from the outside corners of the eyes and the top of the head between ears and down the neck; brush up together, and band or tie it securely.

REMOVING TANGLES

Most of the mats and tangles that you will find on your Yorkshire Terrier will be on the underside or belly. Pet shops sell various conditioners and detangler solutions that can help remove tangles. You can shred part of the mat with your fingers and work it out with a comb. Be patient. If you spend the necessary time brushing every day you should never have to resort to cutting a mat from your dog's coat.

Wrapping the coat of a show dog has two primary purposes: to prevent the hairs' not being damaged by dragging on the floor and to insure the longest possible growth of the hair.

Every part of the dog must be groomed. Tail hairs are often braided.

also avoid getting water in the ear canal. Be prepared for your dog to shake out his coat—you might want to stand back, but make sure you have a hold on the dog to keep him from running through the house.

EAR CLEANING

The ears should be kept clean and any excess hair inside the ear should be trimmed. Ears can be cleaned

skin for any bumps, bites or other abnormalities. Do not neglect any area of the body—get all of the hard-to-reach places.

Once the dog has been thoroughly shampooed, he requires an equally thorough rinsing. Shampoo left in the coat can be irritating to the skin. Protect his eyes from the shampoo by shielding them with your hand and directing the flow of water in the opposite direction. You should

Grooming the Yorkshire Terrier requires patience, skill and plenty of time.

To aid in having the Yorkie remain standing during grooming, a can or tin is used to keep him standing up properly.

with a cotton ball and special cleaner or ear powder made especially for dogs. Be on the lookout for any signs of infection or ear mite infestation. If your Yorkshire Terrier has been shaking his head or scratching at his ears frequently, this usually indicates a problem. If his ears have an unusual odour, this is a sure sign of mite infestation or infection, and a signal to have his ears checked by the veterinary surgeon.

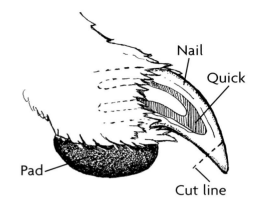

Nail

Quick

Pad

Cut line

Are we finished yet? Can't you just read that in his eyes? The patience of a show Yorkie is legendary.

I'm ready to play now! Such is the life of the show Yorkie. A protective doggy coat can be purchased at quality pet shops or trade stands at dog shows.

NAIL CLIPPING

Your Yorkshire Terrier should be accustomed to having his nails trimmed at an early age, since it will be part of your maintenance routine throughout his life. Not only does it look nicer, but a dog with long nails can cause injury if he jumps up or if he scratches someone unintentionally. Also, a long nail has a better chance of ripping and bleeding, or causing the feet to spread. A good rule of thumb is that if you can hear your dog's nails clicking on the floor when he walks, his nails are too long.

Before you start cutting, make sure you can identify the 'quick' in each nail. The quick is a blood vessel that runs through the centre of each nail and grows rather close to the end. It will bleed if accidentally cut, which will be quite painful for the dog as it contains nerve endings. Keep some type of clotting agent on hand, such as a styptic pencil or styptic powder (the type used for shaving). This will stop the bleeding quickly when applied to the end of the cut nail. Do not panic if this happens, just stop the bleeding and talk soothingly to your dog. Once he has calmed down, move on to the next nail. It is better to clip a little at a time, particularly with black-nailed dogs.

Hold your pup steady as you begin trimming his nails; you do not want him to make any sudden movements or run away. Talk to him soothingly and stroke his fur as you clip. Holding his foot in your hand, simply take off the end of each nail in one quick clip. You can purchase nail clippers that are specially made for dogs; you can probably find them wherever you buy pet or grooming supplies.

The hairs on the bottom of the feet need clipping.

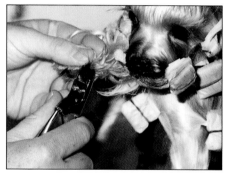

The Yorkie's nails require clipping. Be sure you know how to clip the dog's nail so that you don't make the nail bleed.

DID YOU KNOW?

A dog that spends a lot of time outside on a hard surface such as cement or pavement will have his nails naturally worn down and may not need to have them trimmed as often, except maybe in the colder months when he is not outside as much. Regardless, it is best to get your Yorkie accustomed to this procedure at an early age so that he is used to it. Some dogs are especially sensitive about having their feet touched, but if a dog has experienced it since he was young, he should not be bothered by it.

TRAVELLING WITH YOUR DOG
AUTOMOBILE TRAVEL

You should accustom your Yorkshire Terrier to riding in a car at an early age. You may or may not often take him in the car, but at the very least he will need to go to the vet and you do not want these trips to be traumatic for the dog or a big hassle for you. The safest way for a dog to ride in the car is in his crate. If he uses a fibreglass crate in the house, you can use the same crate for travel. If you have a wire crate in the house, consider purchasing an

77

appropriately sized fibreglass or wooden crate for travelling. Wire crates can be used for travel, but fibreglass or wooden crates are safer.

Put the pup in the crate and see how he reacts. If he seems uneasy, you can have a passenger hold him on his lap while you drive. Another option is a specially made safety harness for dogs, which straps the dog in much like a seat belt. Do not let the dog roam loose in the vehicle—this is very dangerous! If you should stop short, your dog can be thrown and injured. If the dog starts climbing on you and pestering you while you are driving, you will not be able to concentrate on the road. It is an unsafe situation for everyone—human and canine.

For long trips, be prepared to stop to let the dog relieve himself. Bring along whatever you need to clean up after him. You should bring along some old towels and rags, should he have an accident in the car or become carsick.

AIR TRAVEL

If bringing your dog on a flight, you will have to contact the airline to make special arrangements. It is rather common for dogs to travel by air, but advance permission is usually required. The dog will be required to travel in a fibreglass crate; you may be able to use your own or the airline can usually supply one. To help the dog be at ease, put one of his favourite toys in the crate with him. Do not feed the dog for at least six hours before the trip to minimise his need to relieve himself. However, certain regulations specify that water must always be made available to the dog in the crate.

Make sure your dog is properly identified and that your contact information appears on his ID tags and on his crate. Animals travel in a different area of the plane than human passengers, and, although

DID YOU KNOW?
When travelling, never let your dog off-lead in a strange area. Your dog could run away out of fear or decide to chase a passing chipmunk or cat or simply want to stretch his legs without restriction---you might never see your canine friend again.

DID YOU KNOW?
A point that deserves mentioning is never leave your dog alone in the auto. In hot weather your dog can die from the high temperature inside a closed vehicle, and leaving the window open is dangerous as well since the dog can hurt himself trying to get out.

transporting animals is routine for large airlines, there is always that slight risk of getting separated from your dog.

BOARDING
So you want to take a family holiday—and you want to include all members of the family. You would probably

make arrangements for accommodations ahead of time anyway, but this is especially important when travelling with a dog. You do not want to make an overnight stop at the only place around for miles to find out that they do not allow dogs. Also, you do not want to reserve a place for your family without mentioning that you are bringing a dog, because if it is against their policy you may not have a place to stay.

Alternatively, if you are travelling and choose not to bring your Yorkshire Terrier, you

A typical Yorkie carrying-crate is very satisfactory for the car ride or visit to the vet. This crate is not acceptable for airline or tram travel.

DID YOU KNOW?
If your dog gets lost, he is not able to ask for directions home.

Identification tags fastened to the collar give important information—the dog's name, the owner's name, the owner's address and a telephone number where the owner can be reached. This makes it easy for whoever finds the dog to contact the owner and arrange to have the dog returned. An added advantage is that a person will be more likely to approach a lost dog who has ID tags on his collar; it tells the person that this is somebody's pet rather than a stray. This is the easiest and fastest method of identification provided that the tags stay on the collar and the collar stays on the dog.

Your Yorkie should always wear his buckle collar to which his dog tags are attached.

the dogs are kept to make sure that it is clean. Talk to some of the employees and see how they treat the dogs—do they spend time with the dogs, play with them, exercise them, etc.? You know that your Yorkshire Terrier will not be happy unless he gets regular attention. Also find out the kennel's policy on vaccinations and what they require. This is for all of the dogs' safety, since when dogs are kept together, there is a greater risk of diseases being passed from dog to dog. Many veterinary surgeons offer boarding facilities; this is another option.

will have to make arrangements for him while you are away. Some options are to bring him to a neighbour's house to stay while you are gone, to have a

Your Yorkie should wear his collar with ID tags all the time.

trusted neighbour stop by often or stay at your house, or bring your dog to a reputable boarding kennel. If you choose to board him at a kennel, you should stop by to see the facility and where

IDENTIFICATION

Your Yorkshire Terrier is your valued companion and friend. That is why you always keep a close eye on him and you have made sure that he cannot escape from the garden or wriggle out of his collar and run away from you. However, accidents can happen and there may come a time when your dog unexpectedly gets separated from you. If this unfortunate event should occur, the first thing on your mind will be finding him. Proper identification will increase the chances of his being returned to you safely and quickly.

Housebreaking and Training Your Yorkshire Terrier

Living with an untrained dog is a lot like owning a piano that you do not know how to play—it is a nice object to look at but it does not do much more than that to bring you pleasure. Now try taking piano lessons and suddenly the piano comes alive and brings forth magical sounds and rhythms that set your heart singing and your body swaying.

The same is true with your Yorkshire Terrier. At first you enjoy seeing him around the house. He does not do much with you other than to need food, water and exercise. Come to think of it, he does not bring you much joy, either. He is a big responsibility with a very small return. And often, he develops unacceptable behaviours that annoy and/or infuriate you—to say nothing of bad habits that may end up costing you great sums of money. Not a good thing!

Now train your Yorkshire Terrier. Enrol in an obedience class. Teach him good manners as you learn how and why he behaves the way he does. Find out how to communicate with your dog and how to recognise and understand his communications with you. Suddenly the dog takes on a new role in your life—

Your Yorkie is what you make of him. He can be a trained pet or an ill behaved nuisance.

he is smart, interesting, well behaved and fun to be with, and he demonstrates his bond of devotion to you daily. In other words, your Yorkshire Terrier does wonders for your ego because he constantly reminds you that you are not only his leader, you are his hero! Miraculous things have happened—you have a wonderful dog (even your family and friends have noticed the transformation!) and you feel good about yourself.

Those involved with teaching dog obedience and counselling

owners about their dogs' behaviour have discovered some interesting facts about dog ownership. For example, training dogs when they are puppies results in the highest rate of success in developing well-mannered and well-adjusted adult dogs. Training an older dog, say from six months to six years of age, can produce almost equal results providing that the owner accepts the dog's slower rate of learning capability

Puppies are naturally curious and exuberant.

and is willing to work patiently to help the dog succeed at developing to his fullest potential. Unfortunately, the patience factor is what many owners of untrained adult dogs lack, so they do not persist until their dogs are successful at learning particular behaviours.

Training a puppy, for example, aged 8 to 16 weeks (20 weeks at the most) is like working with a dry sponge in a pool of water. The pup soaks up whatever you show him and constantly looks for more things to do and learn. At this early age, his body is not yet producing hormones, and therein lies the reason for such a high rate of suc-

cess. Without hormones, he is focused on his owners and not particularly interested in investigating other places, dogs, people, etc. You are his leader; his provider of food, water, shelter and security. Therefore, he latches onto you and wants to stay close. He will usually follow you from room to room, will not let you out of his sight when you are outdoors with him, and respond in like manner to the people and animals you encounter. If, for example, you greet a friend warmly, he will be happy to greet the person as well. If, however, you are hesitant, even anxious, about the approach of a stranger, he will respond accordingly.

Once the puppy begins to produce hormones, his natural curiosity emerges and he begins to investigate the world around him. It is at that time when you may notice that the untrained dog begins to wander away from you and even ignore your com-

Adolescent Yorkies are as curious as puppies. Their hormonal changes inspire them to investigate every scent around them.

This chapter is devoted to helping you train your Yorkshire Terrier at home. If the recommended procedures are followed faithfully, you may expect positive results that will prove rewarding to both you and your dog.

Whether your Yorkshire Terrier is a puppy or a mature adult, the methods of teaching and the techniques we use in

Frequently the Yorkie will return to his favourite spot at which to urinate. Bowel movements are less consistent though the surface is usually constant. If your Yorkie defecates in grass, he might always insist on grass.

mands to stay close. When this behaviour becomes a problem, the owner has two choices: get rid of the dog or train him. It is strongly urged that you choose the latter option.

Occasionally there are no classes available within a reasonable distance from the owner's home. Sometimes there are classes available but the tuition is too costly. Whatever the circumstances, the solution to the problem of lack of lesson availability lies within the pages of this book.

DID YOU KNOW?

If you have other pets in the home and/or interact often with the pets of friends and other family members,

your pup will respond to those pets in much the same manner as you do. It is only when you show fear or resentment toward another animal that he will act fearful or unfriendly.

DID YOU KNOW?

Mealtime should be a peaceful time for your puppy. Do not put his food and water bowls in a high-traffic area in the house. For example, give him his own little corner of the kitchen where he can eat undisturbed and where he will not be under foot. Do not allow small children or other family members to disrupt the pup when he is eating.

training basic behaviours are the same. After all, no dog, whether puppy or adult, likes harsh or inhumane methods. All creatures, however, respond favourably to gentle motivational methods and sincere praise and encouragement. Now let us get started.

Some Yorkies like stairs, other are afraid of them. Puppies especially cannot use stairs so a ramp can be helpful if your home is elevated.

HOUSEBREAKING

You can train a puppy to relieve itself wherever you choose. For example, city dwellers often train their puppies to relieve themselves in the gutter because large plots of grass are not readily available. Suburbanites, on the other hand, usually have gardens to accommodate their dogs' needs.

Outdoor training includes such surfaces as grass, dirt and cement. Indoor training usually means training your dog to newspaper.

Puppies are naturally curious and exuberant.

When deciding on the surface and location that you will want your Yorkshire Terrier to use, be sure it is going to be permanent. Training your dog to grass and then changing your mind two months later is extremely difficult for both dog and owner.

Next, choose the command you will use each and every time you want your puppy to void. 'Go hurry up' and 'Go make' are examples of commands commonly used by dog owners.

Get in the habit of asking the puppy, 'Do you want to go hurry up?' (or whatever your chosen relief command is) before you take him out. That way, when he becomes an adult, you will be able to determine if he wants to go out when you ask him. A confirmation will be signs of interest, wagging his tail, watching you intently, going to the door, etc.

PUPPY'S NEEDS

Puppy needs to relieve himself after play periods, after each meal, after he has been sleeping and any time he indicates that he is looking for a place to urinate or defecate.

The urinary and intestinal tract muscles of very young puppies are not fully developed. Therefore, like human babies, puppies need to relieve themselves frequently.

Take your puppy out often—every hour for an eight-week-old, for example. The older the puppy, the less often he will need to relieve himself. Finally, as a mature healthy adult, he will require only three to five relief trips per day.

HOUSING

Since the types of housing and control you provide for your puppy has a direct relationship on the success of housetraining, we consider the various aspects of both before we begin training.

Bringing a new puppy home and turning him loose in your house can be compared to turning a child loose in a sports arena and telling the child that the place is all his! The sheer enormity of the place would be too much for him to handle.

Instead, offer the puppy

clearly defined areas where he can play, sleep, eat and live. A room of the house where the family gathers is the most obvious choice. Puppies are social animals and need to feel a part of the pack right from the start. Hearing your voice, watching you while you are doing things and smelling you nearby are all positive reinforcers that he is now a member of your pack. Usually a family room, the

A dog crate is absolutely necessary in the life and training of your Yorkie.

kitchen or a nearby adjoining breakfast area is ideal for providing safety and security for both puppy and owner.

Within that room there should be a smaller area which the puppy can call his own. A cubbyhole, a wire or fibreglass dog crate or a fenced (not boarded!) corner from which he can view the activities of his new family will be fine. The size of the area or crate is the key factor here. The area must be large enough for the puppy to lay down and stretch out as well as

Every Yorkie puppy must have a place to call his own. Pet shops have many kinds of dog beds to offer you.

85

stand up without rubbing his head on the top, yet small enough so that he cannot relieve himself at one end and sleep at the other without coming into contact with his droppings.

Dogs are, by nature, clean animals and will not remain close to their relief areas unless forced to do so. In those cases, they then become dirty dogs and usually remain that way for life.

The crate or cubby should be lined with a clean towel and offer one toy, no more. Do not put food or water in the crate, as eating and drinking will activate his digestive processes and ultimately defeat your purpose as well as make the puppy very uncomfortable as he attempts to 'hold it.'

DID YOU KNOW?
By providing sleeping and resting quarters that fit the dog, and offering frequent opportunities to relieve himself outside his quarters, the puppy quickly learns that the outdoors (or the newspaper if you are training him to paper) is the place to go when he needs to urinate or defecate. It also reinforces his innate desire to keep his sleeping quarters clean. This, in turn, helps develop the muscle control that will eventually produce a dog with clean living habits.

DID YOU KNOW?
Most of all, be consistent. Always take your dog to the same location, always use the same command, and always have him on lead when he is in his relief area, unless a fenced-in garden is available.

By following the recommended method, your puppy will be completely house-trained by the time his muscle and brain development reach maturity. Keep in mind that small breeds usually mature faster than large breeds, but all puppies should be trained by six months of age.

CONTROL
By control, we mean helping the puppy to create a lifestyle pattern that will be compatible to that of his human pack (YOU!). Just as we guide little children to learn our way of life, we must show the puppy when it is time to play, eat, sleep, exercise and even entertain himself.

Your puppy should always sleep in his crate. He should also learn that, during times of household confusion and excessive human activity such as at breakfast when family members are preparing for the day, he can play by himself in relative safety and comfort in his crate. Each time you leave the puppy alone, he should be crated. Puppies are chewers. They cannot tell the difference between lamp cords, television wires,

Canine Development Schedule

It is important to understand how and at what age a puppy develops into adulthood. If you are a puppy owner, consult the following Canine Development Schedule to determine the stage of development your Yorkshire Terrier puppy is currently experiencing. This knowledge will help you as you work with the puppy in the weeks and months ahead.

Period	Age	Characteristics
FIRST TO THIRD	BIRTH TO SEVEN WEEKS	Puppy needs food, sleep and warmth, and responds to simple and gentle touching. Needs mother for security and disciplining. Needs litter mates for learning and interacting with other dogs. Pup learns to function within a pack and learns pack order of dominance. Begin socialising with adults and children for short periods. Begins to become aware of its environment.
FOURTH	EIGHT TO TWELVE WEEKS	Brain is fully developed. Needs socialising with outside world. Remove from mother and littermates. Needs to change from canine pack to human pack. Human dominance necessary. Fear period occurs between 8 and 16 weeks. Avoid fright and pain.
FIFTH	THIRTEEN TO SIXTEEN WEEKS	Training and formal obedience should begin. Less association with other dogs, more with people, places, situations. Period will pass easily if you remember this is pup's change-to-adolescence time. Be firm and fair. Flight instinct prominent. Permissiveness and over-disciplining can do permanent damage. Praise for good behaviour.
JUVENILE	FOUR TO EIGHT MONTHS	Another fear period about 7 to 8 months of age. It passes quickly, but be cautious of fright and pain. Sexual maturity reached. Dominant traits established. Dog should understand sit, down, come and stay by now.

NOTE: THESE ARE APPROXIMATE TIME FRAMES. ALLOW FOR INDIVIDUAL DIFFERENCES IN PUPPIES.

Dogs use crates as a place to get away from it all. Their crate door should always be open when the dog is not in residence.

shoes, table legs, etc. Chewing into a television wire, for example, can be fatal to the puppy while a shorted wire can start a fire in the house.

If the puppy chews on the arm of the chair when he is alone, you will probably discipline him angrily when you get home. Thus, he makes the association that your coming home means he is going to be hit or punished. (He will not remember chewing up the chair and is incapable of making the association of the discipline with his naughty deed.)

THE SUCCESS METHOD
6 Steps to Successful Crate Training

1 Tell the puppy 'Crate time!' and place him in the crate with a small treat (a piece of cheese or half of a biscuit). Let him stay in the crate for five minutes while you are in the same room. Then release him and praise lavishly. Never release him when he is fussing. Wait until he is quiet before you let him out.

2 Repeat Step 1 several times a day.

3 The next day, place the puppy in the crate as before. Let him stay there for ten minutes. Do this several times.

4 Continue building time in five-minute increments until the puppy stays in his crate for 30 minutes with you in the room. Always take him to his relief area after prolonged periods in his crate.

5 Now go back to Step 1 and let the puppy stay in his crate for five minutes, this time while you are out of the room.

6 Once again, build crate time in five-minute increments with you out of the room. When the puppy will stay willingly in his crate (he may even fall asleep!) for 30 minutes with you out of the room, he will be ready to stay in it for several hours at a time.

Other times of excitement, such as family parties, etc., can be fun for the puppy providing he can view the activities from the security of his crate. He is not underfoot and he is not being fed all sorts of titbits that will probably cause him stomach distress, yet he still feels a part of the fun.

Never leave two dogs in the same crate for more than a few minutes.

SCHEDULE

As stated earlier, a puppy should be taken to his relief area each time he is released from his crate, after meals, after a play session, when he first awakens in the morning (at age 8 weeks, this can mean 5 a.m.!) and whenever he indicates by circling or sniffing busily that he needs to urinate or defecate. For a puppy less than ten weeks of age, a routine of taking him out every hour is necessary. As the puppy grows, he will be able to wait for longer periods of time.

Keep trips to his relief area short. Stay no more than five or six minutes and then return to the house. If he goes during that time, praise him lavishly and take him indoors immediately. If he does not, but he has an accident when you go back indoors, pick him up immediately, say 'No! No!' and return to his relief area. Wait a few minutes, then return to the house again. NEVER hit a puppy or rub his face in urine or excrement when he has an accident!

Once indoors, put the puppy in his crate until you have had time to clean up his accident. Then release him to the family area and watch him more closely than before. Chances are, his accident was a result of your not picking up his signal or waiting too long before offering him the opportunity to relieve himself. NEVER hold a grudge against the puppy for accidents.

Let the puppy learn that going outdoors means it is time

Water, which should be readily available, is an absolute MUST for the Yorkshire Terrier.

to relieve himself, not play. Once trained, he will be able to play indoors and out and still differentiate between the times for play versus the times for relief.

Help him develop regular hours for naps, being alone, playing by himself and just resting, all in his crate. Encourage him to

Young Yorkies do not possess the physical ability to control their excretory systems. Frequent trips for relief are necessary until the pups are a five or six months of age.

entertain himself while you are busy with your activities. Let him learn that having you near is comforting, but it is not your main purpose in life to provide him with undivided attention.

Each time you put a puppy in his crate tell him, 'Crate time!' (or whatever command you choose). Soon, he will run to his crate when he hears you say those words.

In the beginning of his training, do not leave him in his crate for prolonged periods of time

Dogs don't sweat. Their tongue is used to cool their blood. Frequent baths help too.

except during the night when everyone is sleeping. Make his experience with his crate a pleasant one and, as an adult, he will

love his crate and willingly stay in it for several hours. There are millions of people who go to work every day and leave their adult dogs crated while they are away. The dogs accept this as their lifestyle and look forward to 'crate time.'

Crate training provides safety for you, the puppy and the home. It also provides the puppy with a feeling of security, and that helps the puppy achieve self-confidence and clean habits.

Remember that one of the primary ingredients in house-training your puppy is control. Regardless of your lifestyle, there will always be occasions when you will need to have a place

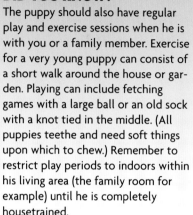

where your dog can stay and be happy and safe. Crate training is the answer for now and in the future.

In conclusion, a few key elements are really all you need for a successful house and crate training method—consistency, frequency, praise, control and supervision. By following these procedures with a normal, healthy puppy, you and the puppy will soon be past the stage of 'accidents' and ready to move on to a full and rewarding life together.

ROLES OF DISCIPLINE, REWARD AND PUNISHMENT

Discipline, training one to act in accordance with rules, brings order to life. It is as simple as that. Without discipline, particularly in a group society, chaos reigns supreme and the group will eventually perish. Humans and canines are social animals and need some form of discipline in order to function effectively. They must procure food, protect their home base and their young and reproduce to keep the species going.

If there were no discipline in the lives of social animals, they would eventually die from starvation and/or predation by other stronger animals.

In the case of domestic canines, dogs need discipline in their lives in order to understand

> **DID YOU KNOW?**
> The puppy should also have regular play and exercise sessions when he is with you or a family member. Exercise for a very young puppy can consist of a short walk around the house or garden. Playing can include fetching games with a large ball or an old sock with a knot tied in the middle. (All puppies teethe and need soft things upon which to chew.) Remember to restrict play periods to indoors within his living area (the family room for example) until he is completely housetrained.

how their pack (you and other family members) function and how they must act in order to survive.

A large humane society in a highly populated area recently surveyed dog owners regarding their satisfaction with their relationships with their dogs. People who had trained their dogs were 75% more satisfied with their pets than those who had never trained their dogs.

Dr. Edward Thorndike, a psychologist, established Thorndike's Theory of Learning, which states that a behaviour that results in a pleasant event tends to be repeated. A behaviour that results in an unpleasant event tends not to be repeated. It

DID YOU KNOW?
Never line your pup's sleeping area with newspaper. Puppy litters are usually raised on newspaper and, once in your home, the puppy will immediately associate newspaper with voiding. Never put newspaper on any floor while housetraining, as this will only confuse the puppy. If you are paper-training him, use paper in his designated relief area ONLY. Finally, restrict water intake after evening meals. Offer a few licks at a time—never let a young puppy gulp water after meals.

is this theory on which training methods are based today. For example, if you manipulate a dog to perform a specific behaviour and reward him for doing it, he is likely to do it again because he enjoyed the end result.

Occasionally, punishment, a penalty inflicted for an offence, is necessary. The best type of punishment often comes from an outside source. For example, a child is told not to touch the stove because he may get burned. He disobeys and touches the stove. In doing so, he receives a burn. From that time on, he respects the heat of the stove and avoids contact with it. Therefore, a behaviour that results in an unpleasant event tends not to be repeated.

A good example of a dog learning the hard way is the dog who chases the house cat. He is told many times to leave the cat alone, yet he persists in teasing the cat. Then, one day he begins chasing the cat but the cat turns and swipes a claw across the dog's face, leaving him with a painful gash on his nose. The final result is that the dog stops chasing the cat.

TRAINING EQUIPMENT
COLLAR
A simple buckle collar is fine for most dogs. One who pulls mightily on the leash may require a chain choker collar. For most Yorkshire Terriers, the basic buckle collar, usually constructed of nylon or cotton, is ideal. The best quality collars can be purchased at a local pet shop, where a wide selection of colours and styles are available.

Yorkies are amongst the most portable of all dogs. These three Yorkshire puppies are too young to train to the lead, so this lovely wicker pram will have to do.

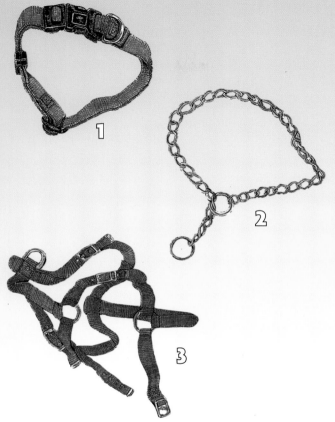

Choose the Right Collar

1 The **BUCKLE or LEATHER COLLAR** is the standard collar used for every day purpose. Be sure that you adjust the buckle on growing puppies. Check it every day. It can become too tight overnight! These collars can be made of leather or nylon. Attach your dog's identification tags to this collar.

2 The **CHOKE CHAIN** is the usual collar recommended for training. It is constructed of highly polished steel so that it slides easily through the stainless steel loop. The idea is that the dog controls the pressure around its neck and he will stop pulling if the collar becomes uncomfortable. Never leave a choke collar on your dog when not training.

3 The **HALTER** is for a trained dog that has to be restrained to prevent running away, chasing a cat and the like. Considered the most humane of all collars, it is frequently used on smaller dogs for which collars are not comfortable.

LEAD

A 1- to 2-metre lead is recommended, preferably made of leather, nylon or heavy cloth. A chain lead is not recommended, as many dog owners find that the chain cuts into their hands and that switching the lead back and forth frequently between their hands is painful.

TREATS

Have a bag of treats on hand. Something nutritious and easy to

Yorkies quickly learn about treats and will react when a treat is offered. Remember that a treat is a reward. By feeding him from the table as you eat, you are merely rewarding him for disturbing you.

DID YOU KNOW?

Taking your dog to an obedience school may be the best investment in time and money you can ever make.  You will enjoy the benefits for the lifetime of your dog and you will have the opportunity to meet people with your own behavioural criteria.

swallow works best; use a soft treat, a chunk of cheese or a piece of cooked chicken rather than a dry biscuit. By the time the dog gets done chewing a dry treat, he will forget why he is being rewarded in the first place! Using food rewards will not teach a dog to beg at the table— the only way to teach a dog to beg at the table is to give him food from the table. In training, rewarding the dog with a food treat away from the table will help him associate praise and the treats with learning new behaviours that obviously please his owner.

DID YOU KNOW?

Do not carry your dog to his toilet area. Lead him there on a leash or, better yet, encourage him to follow you to the spot. If you start carrying him to his spot, you might end up doing this routine forever and your dog will have the satisfaction of having trained YOU.

TRAINING BEGINS: ASK THE DOG A QUESTION

In order to teach your dog anything, you must first get his attention. After all, he cannot learn anything if he is looking away from you with his mind on something else.

To get his attention, ask him, 'School?' and immediately walk over to him and give

DID YOU KNOW?

If you want to be successful in training your dog, you have four rules to obey yourself:
1. Develop an understanding of how a dog thinks.
2. Do not blame the dog for lack of communication.
3. Define your dog's personality and act accordingly.
4. Have patience and be consistent.

him a treat as you tell him 'Good dog.' Wait a minute or two and repeat the routine, this time with a treat in your hand as you approach the dog to within a foot of him. Do not go directly to him, but stop about a foot short of him and hold out the treat as you ask, 'School?' He will see you approaching with a treat in your hand and most likely begin walking

DID YOU KNOW?

Dogs do not understand our language. They can be trained to react to a certain sound, at a certain volume. If you say 'No, Oliver' in a very soft pleasant voice it will not have the same meaning as 'No, Oliver!!' when you shout it as loud as you can. You should never use the dog's name during a reprimand, just the command NO!! Since dogs don't understand words, comics use dogs trained with opposite meanings to the world. Thus, when the comic commands his dog to SIT the dog will stand up; and vice versa.

toward you. As you meet, give him the treat and praise again.

The third time, ask the question, have a treat in your hand and walk only a short distance toward the dog so that he must walk almost all the way to you. As he reaches you, give him the treat and praise again.

By this time, the dog will probably be getting the idea that if he pays attention to you, especially when you ask that question, it will pay off in treats and fun activities for him. In other words, he learns that 'school' means doing fun things with you that result in treats and positive attention for him.

Remember that the dog does not understand your verbal language, he only recognises sounds. Your question translates

to a series of sounds for him, and those sounds become the signal to go to you and pay attention; if he does, he will get to interact with you plus receive treats and praise.

THE BASIC COMMANDS
TEACHING SIT

Now that you have the dog's attention, hold the lead in your left hand and the food treat in your right. Place your food hand at the dog's nose and let him lick the treat but not take it from you.

Training should begin whilst the Yorkie is still a puppy. Dogs must learn that certain behaviour is expected and rewarded.

By the time your Yorkie has matured, he should have mastered the DOWN command.

Say 'Sit' and slowly raise your food hand from in front of the dog's nose up over his head so that he is looking at the ceiling. As he bends his head upward, he will have to bend his knees to maintain his balance. As he bends his knees, he will assume a sit position. At that point, release the food treat and praise lavishly with comments such as 'Good dog! Good sit!', etc. Remember to always praise enthusiastically, because dogs relish verbal praise from their owners and feel so proud of themselves whenever they accomplish a behaviour.

DID YOU KNOW?

Do not issue commands when lying on the floor or lying on your back on the sofa. If you are on your hands and knees when you give a command, your dog will think you are positioning yourself to play.

You will not use food forever in getting the dog to obey your commands. Food is only used to teach new behaviours, and once the dog knows what you want when you give a specific command, you will wean him off of the food treats but still maintain the verbal praise. After all, you will always have your voice with

you, but there will be many times when you have no food rewards yet you expect the dog to obey.

TEACHING DOWN

Teaching the down exercise is easy when you understand how the dog perceives the down position, and it is very difficult when you do not. In addition, teaching the down exercise using the wrong method can sometimes make the dog develop such a fear of the down that he either runs away when you say 'down' or he attempts to bite the person who tries to force him down.

Have the dog sit close alongside your left leg, facing in the same direction as you are. Hold the lead in your left hand and a food treat in your right. Now place your left hand lightly on the top of the dog's shoulders where they meet above the spinal cord. Do not push down on the dog's shoulders; simply rest your left hand there so you can guide the dog to lie down close to your left leg rather than to swing away from your side when he drops.

Now place the food hand at the dog's nose, say 'Down' very softly (almost a whisper), and slowly lower the food hand to the dog's front feet. When the food hand reaches the floor, begin moving it forward along the floor in front of the dog. Keep talking softly to the dog, saying things like, 'Do you want this treat? You can do this, good dog.' Your reassuring tone of voice will help calm the dog as he tries to follow the food hand in order to get the treat.

When the dog's elbows touch the floor, release the food and praise softly. Try to get the dog to maintain that down posi-

tion for several seconds before you let him sit up again. The goal here is to get the dog to settle down and not feel threatened in the down position.

> **DID YOU KNOW?**
> Practice Makes Perfect!
> • Have training lessons with your dog every day in several short segments—three to five times a day for a few minutes at a time is ideal.
> • Do not have long practice sessions. The dog will become easily bored.
> • Never practice when you are tired, ill, worried or in an otherwise negative mood. This will transmit to the dog and may have an adverse effect on its performance.
> Think fun, short and above all POSITIVE! End each session on a high note, rather than a failed exercise, and make sure to give a lot of praise. Enjoy the training and help your dog enjoy it, too.

TEACHING STAY

It is easy to teach the dog to stay in either a sit or a down position. Again, we use food and praise during the teaching process as we help the dog to understand exactly what it is that we are expecting him to do.

To teach the sit/stay, start with the dog sitting on your left side as before and hold the lead in your left hand. Have a food treat in your right hand and place your food hand at the dog's nose. Say 'Stay' and step out on your right foot to stand directly in front of the dog, toe to toe, as he licks and

Teaching the STAY command is difficult for puppies, but far from impossible. Yorkies want to be close to their masters, so it's their natural instinct to follow you.

DID YOU KNOW?

Dogs will do anything for your attention. If you reward the dog when he is calm and resting, you will develop a well-mannered dog. If, on the other hand, you greet your dog excitedly and encourage him to bark and play boisterously with you, the dog will greet you the same way and you will have a hyper dog on your hands.

Within a week or ten days, you can begin to add a bit of distance between you and your dog when you leave him. When you do, use your left hand open with the palm facing the dog as a stay signal, much the same as the hand signal a police officer uses to stop traffic at an intersection. Hold the food treat in your right hand as before, but this time the food is not touching the dog's nose. He will watch the food hand and quickly learn that he is going to get that treat as soon as you return to his side.

Once you get your Yorkie to SIT and STAY you can begin to build time and distance into the discipline and be further away for a longer period of time.

nibbles the treat. Be sure to keep his head facing upward to maintain the sit position. Count to five and then swing around to stand next to the dog again with him on your left. As soon as you get back to the original position, release the food and praise lavishly.

To teach the down/stay, do the down as previously described. As soon as the dog lies down, say 'Stay' and step out on your right foot just as you did in the sit/stay. Count to five and then return to stand beside the dog with him on your left side. Release the treat and praise as always.

When you can stand 1 metre away from your dog for 30 seconds, you can then begin building time and distance in both stays. Eventually, the dog can be expected to remain in the stay position for prolonged periods of time until you return to him or call him to you. Always praise lavishly when he stays.

TEACHING COME

If you make teaching 'Come' a fun experience, you should never have a 'student' that does

DID YOU KNOW?

Dogs are as different from each other as people are. What works for one dog may not work for another. Have an open mind. If one method of training is unsuccessful, try another.

not love the game or that fails to come when called. The secret, it seems, is never to teach the word 'Come.'

At times when an owner most wants his dog to come when called, the owner is likely upset or anxious and he allows these feelings to come through in the tone of his voice when he calls his dog. Hearing that desperation in his owner's voice, the dog fears the results of going to him and therefore either disobeys outright or runs in the opposite direction. The secret, therefore, is to teach the dog a game and, when you want him to come to you, simply play the game. It is practically a no-fail solution!

To begin, have several members of your family take a few food treats and each go into a different room in the house. Take turns calling the dog, and each person should celebrate the dog's finding him with a treat and lots of happy praise. When a person calls the dog, he is actually inviting the dog to find him and get a treat as a reward for 'winning.'

A few turns of the 'Where are you?' game and the dog will figure out that everyone is playing the game and that each person has a big celebration awaiting his success at locating them. Once he learns to love the game, simply calling out 'Where are you?'

> **DID YOU KNOW?**
> When calling the dog, do not say 'Come.' Say things like, 'Rover, where are you? See if you can find me! I have a cookie for you!' Keep up a constant line of chatter with coaxing sounds and frequent questions such as, 'Where are you?' The dog will learn to follow the sound of your voice to locate you and receive his reward.

will bring him running from wherever he is when he hears that all-important question.

The come command is recognised as one of the most important things to teach a dog,

It is easy to teach your dog the COME discipline. The secret is not to use the word come. Call your dog to you only for rewarding reasons. Don't scold or discipline the Yorkie if he successfully comes to you upon command.

so it is interesting to note that there are trainers who work with thousands of dogs and never teach the actual word 'Come.' Yet these dogs will race to respond to a person who uses the dog's name followed by 'Where are you?' In one instance, for example, a woman has a 12-year-old companion dog who went blind, but who never fails to locate her owner

In order for a Yorkshire Terrier to succeed in the show ring, it must master the HEEL command. Proper gaiting requires the dog to move easily at its master's side.

when asked, 'Where are you?'

Children particularly love to play this game with their dogs. Children can hide in smaller places like a shower or bathtub, behind a bed or under a table. The dog needs to work a little bit harder to find these hiding places, but when he does he loves to celebrate with a treat and a tussle with a favourite youngster.

TEACHING HEEL

Heeling means that the dog walks beside the owner without pulling.

Small Yorkie puppies often have a diffi-cult time during the HEEL exercise because they are so small. Do NOT pull on the lead as part of the training.

It takes time and patience on the owner's part to succeed at teaching the dog that he (the owner) will not proceed unless the dog is walking calmly beside him. Pulling out ahead on the lead is definitely not acceptable.

Begin with holding the lead in your left hand as the dog sits beside your left leg. Hold the loop end of the lead in your right hand but keep your left hand short on the lead so it keeps the dog in close next to you.

Say 'Heel' and step forward

DID YOU KNOW?

If you begin teaching the heel by taking long walks and letting the dog pull you along, he misinterprets this action as an acceptable form of taking a walk. When you pull back on the lead to counteract his pulling, he reads that tug as a signal to pull even harder!

---

on your left foot. Keep the dog close to you and take three steps. Stop and have the dog sit next to you in what we now call the 'heel position.' Praise verbally, but do not touch the dog. Hesitate a moment and begin again with 'Heel,' taking three steps and stopping, at which point the dog is told to sit again.

Your goal here is to have the dog walk those three steps with-out pulling on the lead. When he will walk calmly beside you for three steps without pulling, increase the number of steps you take to five. When he will walk politely beside you while you take five steps, you can increase the length of your walk to ten steps. Keep increasing the length of your stroll until the dog will walk quietly beside you without pulling as long as you want him to heel. When you stop heeling, indicate to the dog that the exercise is over by verbally praising as you pet him and say 'OK, good dog.' The 'OK' is used as a release word meaning that the

DID YOU KNOW?

If you start with a normal, healthy dog and give him time, patience and some carefully executed lessons, you will reap the rewards of that training for the life of the dog. And what a life it will be! The two of you will find immeasurable pleasure in the companionship you have built together with love, respect and understanding. Good luck and enjoy!

exercise is finished and the dog is free to relax.

If you are dealing with a dog who insists on pulling you around, simply 'put on your brakes' and stand your ground until the dog realises that the two of you are not going anywhere until he is beside you and moving at your pace, not his. It may take some time just standing there to convince the dog that you are the leader and you will be the one to decide on the direction and speed of your travel.

Each time the dog looks up at you or slows down to give a slack lead between the two of you, quietly praise him and say, 'Good heel. Good dog.' Eventually, the dog will begin to respond and within a few days he will be walking politely beside you without pulling on the lead. At first, the training sessions should be kept short and very positive; soon the dog will be able to

When you stop walking, a properly trained Yorkie will stop and await your next command.

after each exercise. Then, start to give a treat only after every other exercise. Mix up the times when you offer a food reward and the times when you only offer praise so that the dog will never know when he is going to receive both food and praise and when he is going to receive only praise. This

Using food rewards, most trainers agree, is the easiest way to train a dog. Yorkies, like most other dogs, respond positively to this routine bribery!

walk nicely with you for increasingly longer distances. Remember also to give the dog free time and the opportunity to run and play when you are done with heel practice.

WEANING OFF FOOD IN TRAINING
Food is used in training new behaviours, yet once the dog understands what behaviour goes with a specific command, it is time to start weaning him off the food treats. At first, give a treat

is called a variable ratio reward system and it proves successful because there is always the chance that the owner will produce a treat, so the dog never

....And you thought a Yorkie was only a lap dog. Yorkies often compete in advanced levels of obedience training. With patience and consistency, the Yorkie can be trained to do anything!

stops trying for that reward. No matter what, ALWAYS give verbal praise.

OBEDIENCE CLASSES
As previously discussed, it is a good idea to enrol in an obedience class if one is available in your area. Many areas have dog clubs that offer basic obedience training as well as preparatory classes for obedience competition. There are also local dog trainers who offer similar classes.

At obedience trials, dogs can earn titles at various levels of competition. The beginning levels of competition include basic behaviours such as sit, down, heel, etc. The more advanced levels of competition include jumping, retrieving, scent discrimination and signal work. The advanced levels require a dog and owner to put a lot of time and effort into their training; the titles that can be earned at these levels of competition are very prestigious.

DID YOU KNOW?
Dogs are sensitive to their master's moods and emotions. Use your voice wisely when communicating with your dog. Never raise your voice at your dog unless you are angry and trying to correct him. 'Barking' at your dog can become as meaningless as 'dogspeak' is to you. Think before you bark!

DID YOU KNOW?

A dog in jeopardy never lies down. He stays alert on his feet because instinct tells him that he may have to run away or fight for his survival. Therefore, if a dog feels threatened or anxious, he will not lie down. Consequently, it is important to have the dog calm and relaxed as he learns the down exercise.

OTHER ACTIVITIES FOR LIFE

Whether a dog is trained in the structured environment of a class or alone with his owner at home, there are many activities that can bring fun and rewards to both owner and dog once they have mastered basic control.

Teaching the dog to help out around the home, in the garden or on the farm provides great satisfaction to both dog and owner.

In addition, the dog's help makes life a little easier for his owner and raises his stature as a valued companion to his family. It helps give the dog a purpose; it helps to keep his mind occupied and provides an outlet for his energy.

If you are interested in participating in organised competition with your Yorkshire Terrier, there are other activities other than obedience in which you and your dog can become involved. Agility is a popular and fun sport where dogs run through an obstacle course that includes various jumps, tunnels and other exercises to test the dog's speed and coordination. The owners often run through the course beside their dogs to give commands and to guide them through the course. Although competitive, the focus is on fun—it's fun to do and fun to watch, as well as great exercise.

Yes, Yorkies are small, but they have tremendous brain power and a strong desire to please. With these characteristics in your arsenal, you should be able to train your dog for agility trials.

HOW MANY TIMES A DAY?

AGE	RELIEF TRIPS
To 14 weeks	10
14–22 weeks	8
22–32 weeks	6
Adulthood	4
(dog stops growing)	

These are estimates, of course, but they are a guide as to the MINIMUM opportunities a dog should have each day to relieve itself.

Crate training is extremely important in the life of a Yorkie. For the protection of your Yorkie, the crate is the safest refuge he will know. In addition to being the best aid in training and housebreaking, crates are ideal for travelling to a dog show, the vet's office or your holiday destination.

Health Care of Your Yorkshire Terrier

Dogs, being mammals like human beings, suffer many of the same physical illnesses as people. They might even share many of the psychological problems. Since people usually know more about human diseases than canine maladies, many of the terms used in this chapter will be the familiar terms, not necessarily those used by veterinary surgeons. We'll still use the term X-RAY, instead of the more acceptable term RADIOGRAPH. We will also use the familiar term SYMPTOMS even though dogs don't have symptoms, dogs have CLINICAL SIGNS. SYMPTOMS, by the way, are verbal descriptions of the patient's feelings. Since dogs can't speak, we have to look for clinical signs...but we still use the term SYMPTOMS in this book.

As a general rule, medicine is PRACTISED. That term is not arbitrary. Medicine is an art. It is a constantly changing art as we learn more and more about genetics, electronic aids (like CAT scans) and opinions. There are many dog maladies, like canine hip dysplasia, which are not universally treated in the same manner. Some veterinary surgeons opt for surgery more often than others.

SELECTING A VETERINARY SURGEON
Your selection of a veterinary surgeon should not be based upon personality (as most are) but upon their convenience to your home. You want a doctor who is close as you might have emergencies or multiple visits for treatments. You want a doctor who has services that you might require such as grooming facilities, who makes sophisticated pet supplies available and who has a good reputation for ability and responsiveness. There is nothing more frustrating than having to wait a day or more to get a response from a veterinary surgeon.

Select your veterinary surgeon based upon proximity to your home and recommendations from other dog owners.

All veterinary surgeons are licensed and their diplomas and/or certificates should be displayed in their waiting rooms. There are, however, many veterinary specialties which usually require further studies and internships. There are specialists in heart problems (veterinary cardiologists), skin problems (veterinary dermatologists), teeth and gum problems (veterinary dentists), eye problems (veterinary ophthalmologists), x-rays (veterinary radiologists), and surgeons who have specialties in bones, muscles or other organs. Most veterinary surgeons do routine surgery such as neutering, stitching up wounds and docking tails for those breeds in which such is required for show purposes. When the problem affecting your dog is serious, it is not unusual or impudent to get another medical opinion. You might also want to compare costs between several veterinary surgeons. Sophisticated health care and veterinary services can be very costly. Don't be bashful to discuss these costs with your veterinary surgeon or his (her) staff. It is not infrequent that important decisions are based upon financial considerations.

PREVENTATIVE MEDICINE

It is much easier, less costly and more effective to practice preventative medicine than to fight bouts of illness and disease.

Properly bred puppies come from parents that were selected based upon their genetic disease profile. Their mothers should have been vaccinated, free of all internal and external parasites, and properly nourished. For these reasons, a visit to the veterinary surgeon who cared for the dam (mother) is recommended. The dam can pass on disease

Your vet should give your Yorkie puppy a thorough examination as soon after you get it as possible. If there is a medical problem it should be treated immediately or the puppy should be returned to the breeder.

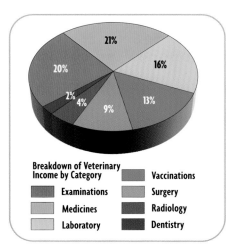

Breakdown of Veterinary Income by Category
- Examinations
- Medicines
- Laboratory
- Vaccinations
- Surgery
- Radiology
- Dentistry

A typical American vet's income categorised according to services performed. This survey dealt with small-animal (pets) practices.

MEDICAL PROBLEMS
MOST FREQUENTLY SEEN IN YORKSHIRE TERRIERS

Condition	Age Affected	Cause	Area Affected
Cataracts	3 to 6 years	Congenital	Lens of the eyes
Collapsed Trachea	Adult	Possibly congenital or diet	Upper trachea
Cryptorchidism	Birth (by 4 months)	Congenital	Testicle(s)
Elbow Dysplasia	1 to 2 years	Congenital	Elbow joint
Hip Dysplasia	By 2 years	Congenital	Hip joint
Hypoglycemia	Birth	Possbily congenital	Blood
Hypothyroidism	1 to 3 years	Lymphocytic throiditis	Endocrine system
Keratoconjunctivitis Sicca	Adult	Congenital/immunological	Tear ducts of eyes
Legg-Calve-Perthes Disease	4 to 12 months	Congenital	Leg
Medial Patellar Luxation	Any age	Congenital	Knee cap
Progressive Retinal Atrophy	5 to 11 years	Congenital	Retinal tissue of eyes
Ulcerative Keratitis	Any age	Irritating hairs (on eyes)	Surface of cornea
Valvular Insufficiency	7 to 8 years	Possibly congenital	Heart valves
Vertebral Malformation	Less than 1 year	Unknown	Spinal cord
Von Willebrand's Disease	Birth	Congenital	Blood

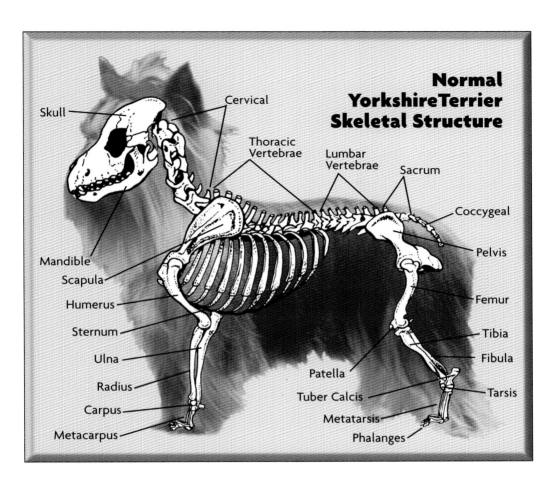

Normal Yorkshire Terrier Skeletal Structure

Skull

Cervical

Thoracic Vertebrae

Lumbar Vertebrae

Sacrum

Coccygeal

Pelvis

Mandible

Scapula

Humerus

Sternum

Ulna

Radius

Carpus

Metacarpus

Femur

Tibia

Fibula

Patella

Tuber Calcis

Metatarsis

Phalanges

Tarsis

resistance to her puppies. This resistance can last for 8–10 weeks. She can also pass on parasites and many infections. That's why you should visit the veterinary surgeon who cared for the dam.

WEANING TO FIVE MONTHS OLD
Puppies should be weaned by the time they are about two months old. A puppy that remains for at least eight weeks with its mother and litter mates usually adapts

The dam's milk immunises a puppy for eight to ten weeks.

better to other dogs and people later in its life.

In every case, you should have your newly acquired puppy examined by a veterinary surgeon immediately. Vaccination programmes usually begin when the puppy is very young.

The puppy will have its teeth examined, have its skeletal conformation checked, and have its general health checked prior to certification by the veterinary surgeon. Many puppies have problems with their knee caps, eye cataracts and other eye problems, heart murmurs and undescended testicles. They may also have personality problems and your veterinary surgeon might have training in temperament evaluation.

Your veterinary surgeon should schedule vaccinations. Keep a record yourself.

VACCINATION SCHEDULING

Most vaccinations are given by injection and should only be done by a veterinary surgeon. Both he and you should keep a record of the date of the injection, the identifica-

> **DID YOU KNOW?**
> Your veterinary surgeon will probably recommend that your puppy be vaccinated before you take him outside. There are airborne diseases, parasite eggs in the grass and unexpected visits from other dogs that might be dangerous to your puppy's health.

> **DID YOU KNOW?**
> Ridding your puppy of worms is VERY IMPORTANT because certain worms that puppies carry can infect humans, such as tapeworms, hookworms and roundworms.
>
> Since puppies are never housebroken at two to three weeks of age, it is easy for them to pass on the parasites (worms) to humans.
>
> Breeders initiate a deworming programme two weeks after weaning. The routine is repeated every two or three weeks until the puppy is three months old. The breeder from whom you obtained your puppy should provide you with the complete details of the deworming programme.
>
> Your veterinary surgeon can prescribe and monitor the programme of deworming for you. The usual programme is treating the puppy every 15–20 days until the puppy is positively worm free.
>
> It is not advised that you treat your puppy with drugs which are not recommended professionally.

tion of the vaccine and the amount given. The vaccination scheduling is based on a 15-day cycle. The first vaccinations should start when the puppy is 6-8 weeks old, then 15 days later when it is 10-12 weeks of age and later when it is 14-16 weeks of age. Vaccinations should NEVER be given without a 15-day lapse between injections. Most vaccinations immunise your puppy against viruses.

HEALTH AND VACCINATION SCHEDULE

AGE IN WEEKS:	3RD	6TH	8TH	10TH	12TH	14TH	16TH	20-24TH
Worm Control	✔	✔	✔	✔	✔	✔	✔	✔
Neutering								✔
Heartworm		✔						✔
Parvovirus		✔		✔		✔		✔
Distemper			✔		✔		✔	
Hepatitis			✔		✔		✔	
Leptospirosis		✔		✔		✔		
Parainfluenza		✔		✔		✔		
Dental Examination			✔					✔
Complete Physical			✔					✔
Temperament Testing			✔					
Coronavirus					✔			
Canine Cough		✔						
Rabies								✔

Vaccinations are not instantly effective. It takes about two weeks for the dog's immunisation system to develop antibodies. Most vaccinations require annual booster shots. Your veterinary surgeon should guide you in this regard.

The usual vaccines contain immunising doses of several different viruses such as distemper, parvovirus, parainfluenza and hepatitis. There are other vaccines available when the puppy is at risk. You should rely upon professional advice. This is especially true for the booster shot programme. Most vaccination programmes require a booster when the puppy is a year old, and once a year thereafter. In some cases, circumstances may require more frequent immunisations.

Kennel cough, more formally known as tracheobronchitis, is treated with a vaccine which is sprayed into the dog's nostrils.

DID YOU KNOW?
Caring for the puppy starts before the puppy is born by keeping the dam healthy and well-nourished. When the puppy is about three weeks old, it must start its disease-control regimen. The first treatments will be for worms. Most puppies have worms, even if they are tested negative for worms. The test essentially is checking the stool specimens for the eggs of the worms. The worms continually shed eggs except during their dormant stage, when they just rest in the tissues of the puppy. During this stage they don't shed eggs and are not evident during a routine examination.

The effectiveness of a parvovirus vaccination programme can be tested to be certain that the vaccinations are protective. Your veterinary surgeon will explain and manage all of these details.

Skin problems can be caused by contact with chemicals or other irritants. It is called contact dermatitis.

FIVE MONTHS TO ONE YEAR OF AGE

By the time your puppy is five months old, he should have completed his vaccination programme. During his physical examination he should be evaluated for the common hip dysplasia plus other diseases of the joints. There are tests to assist in the prediction of these problems. Other tests can also be run, such as the parvovirus antibody titer, which can assess the effectiveness of the vaccination programme.

Unless you intend to breed or show your dog, neutering the puppy at six months of age is recommended. Discuss this with your veterinary surgeon.

By the time your Yorkshire Terrier is seven or eight months of age, he can be seriously evaluated for his conformation to the club standard, thus determining its show potential and its desirability as a sire or dam. If the puppy is

DID YOU KNOW?

As Yorkie puppies become more and more expensive, especially those puppies of high quality for showing and/or breeding, they have a greater chance of being stolen. The usual collar dog tag is, of course, easily removed. But there are two techniques which are becoming widely utilised for identification.

The puppy microchip implantation involves the injection of a small microchip, about the size of a corn kernel, under the skin of the dog. If your dog shows up at a clinic or shelter, or is offered for resale under less than savory circumstances, it can be positively identified by the microchip. The microchip is scanned and a registry quickly identifies you as the owner. This is not only protection against theft, but should the dog run away or go chasing a varmint and get lost, you have a fair chance of getting it back.

Tattooing is done on various parts of the dog, from its belly to its cheeks. The number tattooed can be your telephone number or any other number which you can easily memorise. When professional dog thieves see a tattooed dog, they usually lose interest in it. Both microchipping and tattooing can be done at your local veterinary clinic. For the safety of our Yorkies, no laboratory facility or dog broker will accept a tattooed dog as stock.

not top class and therefore is not a candidate for a serious breeding programme, most professionals advise neutering the puppy. Neutering has proven to be extremely beneficial to both male and female puppies. Besides the obvious impossibility of pregnancy, it inhibits (but does not prevent) breast cancer in bitches and prostate cancer in male dogs.

Blood tests are performed for heartworm infestation and it is possible that your puppy will be placed on a preventative therapy which will prevent heartworm infection as well as control other internal parasites.

Serious skin and coat problems require the attention of a veterinary dermatologist.

DOGS OLDER THAN ONE YEAR
Continue to visit the veterinary surgeon at least once a year. There is no such disease as old age, but bodily functions do change with age, and the eyes and ears are no longer as efficient. Neither are the internal workings of the liver, kidneys and intestines. Proper dietary changes, recommended by your veterinary surgeon, can make life more pleasant for the ageing Yorkshire Terrier and you.

SKIN PROBLEMS IN YORKSHIRE TERRIERS

Veterinary surgeons are consulted by dog owners for skin problems more than any other group of diseases or maladies. Dogs' skin is almost as sensitive as human skin and both suffer almost the same ailments. (Though the occurrence of acne in dogs is rare!) For this reason, veterinary dermatology has developed into a specialty practiced by many vets.

Since many skin problems have visual symptoms which are almost identical, it requires the skill of an experienced veterinary dermatologist to identify and cure many of the more severe skin disorders. Simply put, if your dog is suffering from a skin disorder, seek professional assistance as quickly as possible. As with all diseases, the earlier a problem is identified and treated, the more successful is the cure.

Pet shops sell many treatments for skin problems. Most of the treatments are simply directed at symptoms and not the underlying problem(s).

AUTO-IMMUNE SKIN CONDITIONS

Auto-immune skin conditions are commonly referred to as being allergic to yourself. Allergies, though, usually result in inflammatory reactions to an outside stimulus. Auto-immune diseases cause serious damage to the tissues which are involved.

The best known auto-immune disease is lupus. It affects people as well as dogs. The symptoms are very variable and may affect the kidneys, bones, blood chemistry and skin. It can be fatal to both dogs and humans, though it is not thought to be transmissible. It is usually successfully treated with cortisone, prednisone or similar corticosteroid, but extensive use of these drugs can have harmful side effects.

INHERITED SKIN PROBLEMS

Many skin disorders are inherited and some are fatal.

DID YOU KNOW?

There is a 4:1 chance of a puppy getting this fatal gene combination from two parents with recessive genes for acrodermatitis:

AA= NORMAL, HEALTHY
aa= FATAL
Aa= RECESSIVE, NORMAL APPEARING

If the female parent has an Aa gene and the male parent has an Aa gene, the chances are one in four that the puppy will have the fatal genetic combination aa.

Dam

		A	a	♀
Sire	A	AA	Aa	
	a	Aa	aa	
	♂			

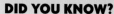

Acrodermatitis is an inherited disease which is transmitted by BOTH parents. The parents, which appear (phenotypically) normal, have a recessive gene for acrodermatitis, meaning that they carry, but are not affected by the disease.

    Acrodermatitis is just one example of how difficult it is to

DID YOU KNOW?
Chances are that you and your dog will have the same allergies. Your allergies are readily recognizable and usually easily treated. Your dog's allergies may be masked

Disease	What is it?	What causes it?	Symptoms
Leptospirosis	Severe disease that affects the internal organs; can be spread to people.	A bacterium, which is often carried by rodents, that enters through mucous membranes and spreads quickly throughout the body.	Range from fever, vomiting and loss of appetite in less severe cases to shock, irreversible kidney damage and possibly death in most severe cases.
Rabies	Potentially deadly virus that infects warm-blooded mammals. Not seen in United Kingdom.	A bacterium, which is often carried by rodents, that enters through mucous membranes and spreads quickly throughout the body.	1st stage: dog exhibits change in behaviour, fear. 2nd stage: dog's behaviour becomes more aggressive. 3rd stage: loss of coordination, trouble with bodily functions.
Parvovirus	Highly contagious virus, potentially deadly.	Ingestion of the virus, which is usually spread through the faeces of infected dogs.	Most common: severe diarrhoea. Also vomiting, fatigue, lack of appetite.
Kennel cough	Contagious respiratory infection.	Combination of types of bacteria and virus. Most common: *Bordetella bronchiseptica* bacteria and parainfluenza virus.	Chronic cough.
Distemper	Disease primarily affecting respiratory and nervous system.	Virus that is related to the human measles virus.	Mild symptoms such as fever, lack of appetite and mucous secretion progress to evidence of brain damage, 'hard pad.'
Hepatitis	Virus primarily affecting the liver.	Canine adenovirus type I (CAV-1). Enters system when dog breathes in particles.	Lesser symptoms include listlessness, diarrhoea, vomiting. More severe symptoms include 'blue-eye' (clumps of virus in eye).
Coronavirus	Virus resulting in digestive problems.	Virus is spread through infected dog's faeces.	Stomach upset evidenced by lack of appetite, vomiting, diarrhoea.

diagnose and treat many dog diseases. The cost and skills required to ascertain whether two dogs should be mated is too high even though puppies with acrodermatitis rarely reach two years of age.

Other inherited skin problems are usually not as fatal

DID YOU KNOW?
Vaccines do not work all the time. Sometimes dogs are allergic to them and many times the antibodies, which are supposed to be stimulated by the

vaccine, just are not produced. You should keep your dog in the veterinary clinic for an hour after it is vaccinated to be sure there are no allergic reactions.

as acrodermatitis. All inherited diseases must be diagnosed and treated by a veterinary special-ist. There are active programmes being undertaken by many veterinary pharmaceutical manufacturers to solve most, if not all, of the common skin problems of dogs.

PARASITE BITES
Many of us are allergic to mosqui-to bites. The bites itch, erupt and may even become infected. Dogs have the same reaction to fleas, ticks and/or mites. When you feel the prick of the mosquito when it bites you, you have a chance to kill it with your hand. Unfortunately, when our dog is bitten by a flea, tick or mite, it can only scratch it away or bite it. By the time the dog has been bitten, the parasite has done some of its damage. It may also have laid eggs to cause further problems in the near future. The itching from parasite bites is probably due to the saliva injected into the site when the parasite sucks the dog's blood.

AIRBORNE ALLERGIES
Another interesting allergy is pollen allergy. Humans have hay fever, rose fever and other fevers with which they suffer during the pollinating season. Many dogs suffer the same allergies. So when the pollen count is high, your dog might suffer. Don't expect them to sneeze and have runny noses like humans. Dogs react to pollen allergies the same way they react to fleas—they scratch and bite themselves. Yorkshire Terriers are very susceptible to airborne pollen allergies.

Dogs, like humans, can be tested for allergens. Discuss the testing with your veterinary derma-tologist.

FOOD ALLERGIES

Dogs are allergic to many foods which are best-sellers and highly recommended by breeders and veterinary surgeons. Changing the brand of food that you buy may not eliminate the problem because the element of the food to which the dog is allergic may also be contained in the new brand.

Recognizing a food allergy is difficult. Humans vomit or have rashes when they eat a food to which they are allergic. Dogs neither vomit nor (usually) develop a rash. Instead they itch, scratch and bite, thus making the diagnosis extremely difficult. While pollen allergies and parasite bites are usually seasonal, food allergies are year-round problems.

TREATING FOOD PROBLEMS

Handling food allergies and food intolerance yourself is possible. Put your dog on a diet which it has never had. Obviously if it has never eaten this new food it can't have been allergic or intolerant of it. Start with a single ingredient which is NOT in the dog's diet at the present time. Ingredients like chopped beef or fish are common in dog's diets, so try something more exotic like ostrich, rabbit, pheasant or even just vegetables such as potatoes. Keep the dog on this diet (with no additives) for a month. If the symptoms of food allergy or intolerance disappear,

chances are that you have defined the cause.

Don't think that the single ingredient cured the problem. You still must find a suitable diet and ascertain which ingredient in the old diet was objectionable. This is most easily done by adding ingredients to the new diet one at a time until the problem is solved.

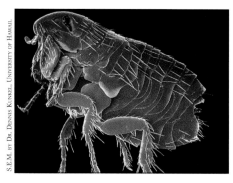

An S.E.M. (scanning electron micrograph), magnified and computer coloured, of a dog flea, *Ctenocephalides canis.*

S.E.M. BY DR. DENNIS KUNKEL, UNIVERSITY OF HAWAII.

Let the dog stay on the modified diet for a month before you add another ingredient.

An alternative method is to carefully study the ingredients in the diet to which your dog is allergic or intolerant. Identify the main ingredient in this diet and eliminate the main ingredient by buying a different food which does not have that ingredient. Keep experimenting until the symptoms disappear after one month on the new diet.

EXTERNAL PARASITES

Of all the problems to which dogs are prone, none is more well

The magnified image of a male dog flea, *Ctenocephalides canis*.

Photo by Jean Claude Revy/Phototake

(opposite page) A scanning electron micrograph of a dog or cat flea, *Ctenocephalides felis*, enlarged, magnified and coloured for effect.

known and frustrating than fleas. Fleas, which usually refers to fleas, ticks and mites, are relatively simple to cure but difficult to prevent. The opposite is true for the parasites which are harboured inside the body. They are a bit more difficult to cure but they are easier to control.

Dog flea eggs magnified.

FLEAS
It is possible to control flea infestation but you have to understand the life cycle of a typical flea in order to control them. Basically fleas are a

Male cat flea, *Ctenocephalides felis*, commonly found on dogs as well as cats.

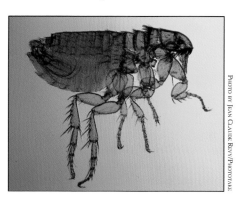

Photo by Jean Claude Revy/Phototake

The Life Cycle of the Flea

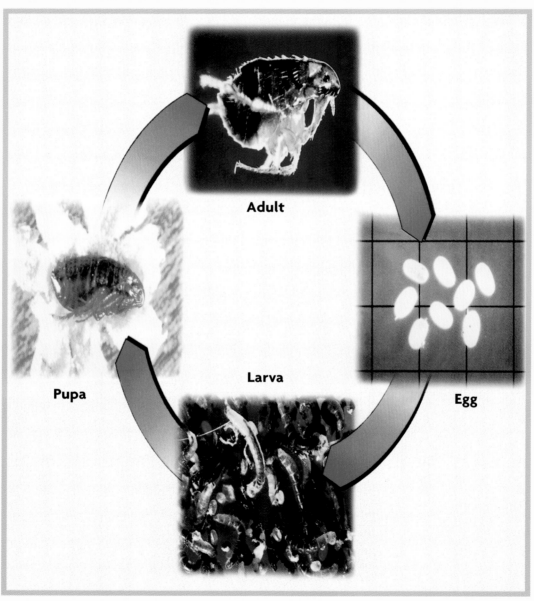

The Life Cycle of the Flea was posterized by Fleabusters. Poster courtesy of Fleabusters®, Rx for Fleas.

PHOTO BY DWIGHT R. KUHN

Several species infest both dog and cats. The dog flea is scientifically known as *Ctenocephalides canis* while the cat flea is *Ctenocephalides felis*. Cat fleas are very common on dogs.

Fleas lay eggs while they are in residence on your dog. These eggs do not adhere to the hair of your dog and they simply fall off almost as soon as they dry (they may be a bit damp when initially laid). These eggs are the reservoir of future flea infestations. If your dog scratches himself and is able

An exceptional action photo showing a flea jumping from a dog's back.

Yorkies can pick up fleas, ticks and worm eggs from the outdoors.

summertime problem and their effective treatment (destruction) is environmental. The problem is that there is no single flea control medicine (insecticide) which can be used in every flea infested area. To understand flea control you must apply suitable treatment to the weak link in the life cycle of the flea.

THE LIFE CYCLE OF A FLEA

Fleas are found in four forms: eggs, larvae, pupae and adults. You really need a low-power microscope or hand lens to identify a living flea's eggs, pupae or larva. They spend their whole lives on your Yorkshire Terrier unless they are forcibly removed by brushing, bathing, scratching or biting.

to dislodge a few fleas, they simply fall off and await a future chance to attack a dog...or even a person. Yes, fleas from dogs bite people. That's why it is so

The head of the dog flea, *Ctenocephalides canis*, magnified by a scanning electron micrograph.

S.E.M. BY DR. DENNIS KUNKEL, UNIVERSITY OF HAWAII.

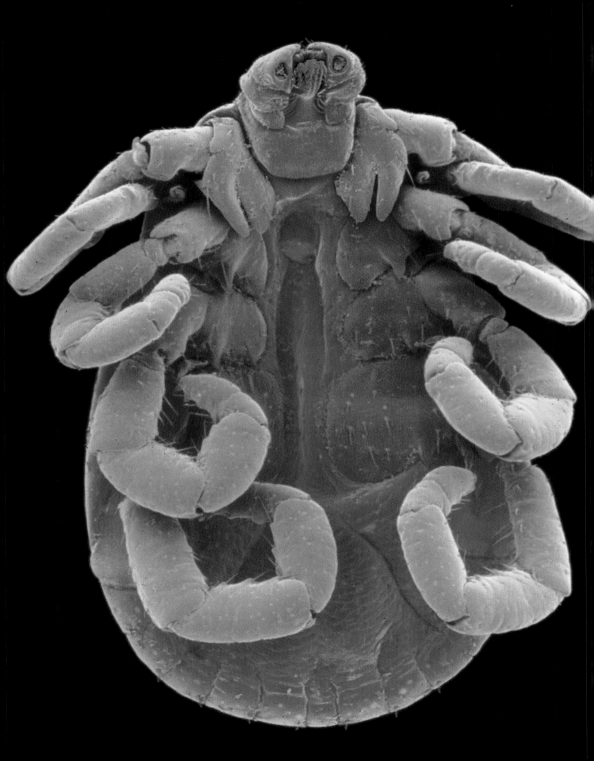

Photo by Dwight R. Kuhn

A photo of a human louse. It's very difficult to differentiate between lice from humans and lice from dogs.

(opposite page) The dog tick, *Dermacentor variabilis*, is the most common tick found on dogs. Look at the eight legs! No wonder ticks are difficult to remove.

Don't forget cupboards, under furniture, cushions. A study has reported that a vacuum cleaner with a beater bar can only remove 20% of the larvae and 50% of the eggs. The vacuum bags should be discarded into a sealed plastic bag or burned. The vacuum machine itself should be cleaned. The outdoor area to which your dog has access must also be treated with an insecticide.

Your vet will be able to recommend a household insecticidal spray but this must be used with caution and instructions strictly adhered to.

While there are many drugs available to kill fleas on the dog itself, such as the miracle drug ivermectin, it is best to have the de-fleaing and de-worming

important to control fleas both on the dog and in the dog's entire environment. You must, therefore, treat the dog and the environment simultaneously.

DE-FLEAING THE HOME

Cleanliness is the simple rule. If you have a cat living with your dog, the matter is more complicated since most dog fleas are actually cat fleas. But since cats climb onto many areas that are never accessible to dogs (like window sills, table tops, etc.), you have to clean all of these areas, too. The hard floor surfaces (tiles, wood, stone and linoleum) must be mopped several times a day. Drops of food onto the floor are actually food for flea larvae! All rugs and furniture must be vacuumed several times a day.

Ticks can only live by ingesting blood.

supervised by your vet. Ivermectin is effective against many external and internal parasites including heartworms, roundworms, tapeworms, flukes, ticks and mites. It has not been approved for use to control these pests, but veterinary surgeons frequently use it anyway. Ivermectin may not be available in all areas.

123

The mange mite, *Psoroptes bovis*, magnified more than 200 times.

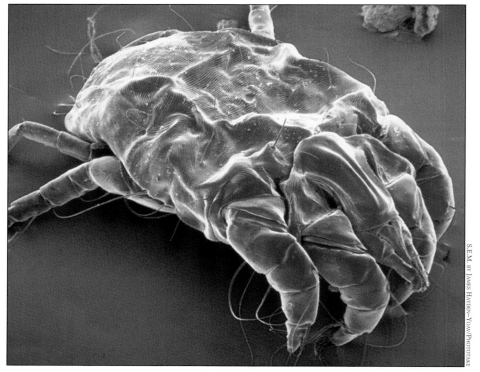

S.E.M. BY JAMES HAYDEN–YOAV/PHOTOTAKE

STERILISING THE ENVIRONMENT

Besides cleaning your home with vacuum cleaners and mops, you have to treat the outdoor range of your dog. This means trimming bushes, spreading insecticide and being careful not to poison areas in which fishes or other animals reside.

This is best done by an outside service specialising in de-fleaing. Your vet should be able to recommend a local service.

TICKS AND MITES

Though not as common as fleas, ticks and mites are found all over the tropical and temperate world. They don't bite, like fleas, rather they harpoon. They dig their sharp proboscis (nose) into the dog's skin and drink the blood. Their only food and drink is dog's blood. Dogs can get Lyme disease, Rocky Mountain spotted fever (normally found in the U.S.A. only), paralysis and many other diseases, from ticks and mites. They may live where fleas are found except they like to hide in cracks or seams in walls wherever dogs live. They are controlled the same way fleas are controlled.

The dog tick *Dermacentor*

variabilis may well be the most common dog tick in many geographical areas, especially those areas where the climate is hot and humid.

Most dog ticks have life expectancies of a week to six months, depending upon climatic conditions. They can neither jump nor fly, but they can crawl slowly and can range up to 5 metres (16 feet) to reach a sleeping or unsuspecting dog.

The head of the dog tick, *Dermacentor variabilis*, magnified and colourised.

S.E.M. BY DR. DENNIS KUNKEL, UNIVERSITY OF HAWAII.

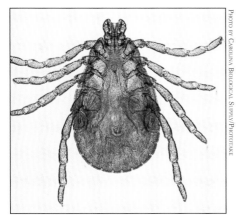

PHOTO BY CAROLINA BIOLOGICAL SUPPLY/PHOTOTAKE

A brown dog tick, *Rhipicephalus sanguineus.*

INTERNAL PARASITES

Most animals—fishes, birds and mammals, including dogs and humans—have worms and other parasites which live inside their bodies. According to Dr. Herbert R. Axelrod, the fish pathologist, there are two kinds of parasites: dumb and smart. The smart parasites live in peaceful coopera-

MANGE

Mites cause a skin irritation called mange. Some are contagious, like *Cheyletiella*, ear mites, scabies and chiggers. The non-contagious mites are *Demodex*. The most serious of the mites is the ear mite infestation. Ear mites are usually controlled with ivermectin.

It is essential that your dog be treated for mange as quickly as possible because some forms of mange are transmissible to people.

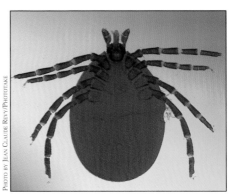

PHOTO BY JEAN CLAUDE REVY/PHOTOTAKE

An uncommon dog tick of the genus *Ixode*, magnified and colourised.

125

DID YOU KNOW?

There are many parasiticides which can be used around your home and garden to control fleas.

• Natural pyrethrins can be used inside the house.

• Allethrin, bioallethrin, permethrin and resmethrin can also be used inside the house but permethrin has been used success-fully outdoors, too.

• Carbaryl can be used indoors and outdoors.

• Propxur can be used indoors.

• Chlorpyrifos, diazinon and malathion can be used indoors or outdoors and it has an extended residual activity.

tion with their hosts (symbiosis), while the dumb parasites kill their host. Most of the worm infections are relatively easy to control. If they are not controlled they eventually weaken the host dog to the point that other medical problems occur, but they are not dumb parasites.

ROUNDWORMS

The roundworms that infect dogs are scientifically known as *Toxocara canis*. They live in the dog's intestine. The worms shed eggs continually. It has been estimated that a dog produces about 150 grammes of faeces every day. Each gramme of faeces averages 10,000-12,000 eggs of

The roundworm, *Ascaris lumbricoides*.

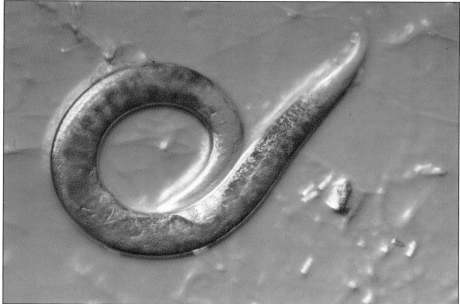

PHOTO BY CAROLINA BIOLOGICAL SUPPLY/PHOTOTAKE

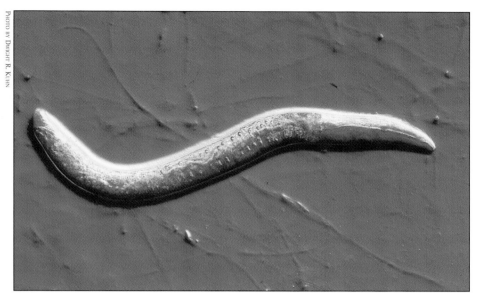

Photo by Dwight R. Kuhn

The roundworm, *Ascaris lumbricoides*, infects humans, dogs and pigs.

roundworms. There are no known areas in which dogs roam that does not contain the eggs of roundworms. The greatest danger of roundworms is that they infect people, too! It is wise to have your dog tested regularly for roundworms.

Pigs also have roundworm infections which can be passed to human and dogs. The typical pig roundworm parasite is called *Ascaris lumbricoides.*

HOOKWORMS
The worm *Ancylostoma caninum* is commonly called the dog hookworm. It is dangerous to humans and cats. It also has teeth by which it attaches itself to the intestines of the dog. Because it changes the site of its attachment

DID YOU KNOW?
Humans, rats, squirrels, foxes, coyotes, wolves, mixed breeds of dogs and purebred dogs are all susceptible to tapeworm infection. Except in humans, tapeworms are usually not a fatal infection. Infected individuals can harbour a thousand parasitic worms. Tapeworms have two sexes—male and female (many other worms have only one sex—male and female in the same worm). If dogs eat infected rats or mice, they get the tapeworm disease. One month after attaching to a dog's intestine, the worm starts shedding eggs. These eggs are infective immediately. Infective eggs can live for a few months without a host animal.

127

The roundworm, *Rhabditis*.

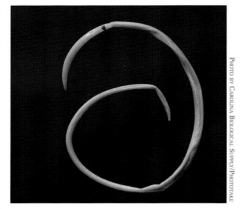

PHOTO BY CAROLINA BIOLOGICAL SUPPLY/PHOTOTAKE

Male and female hookworms, *Ancylostoma caninum*, very rarely infect Yorkshire Terriers.

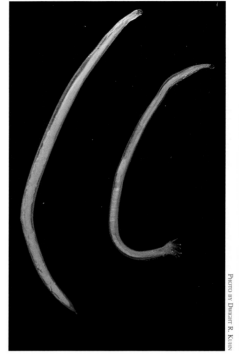

PHOTO BY DWIGHT R. KUHN

DID YOU KNOW?

Ivermectin is quickly becoming the drug of choice for treating many parasitic skin diseases in dogs.

For some unknown reason, herding dogs like Collies, Old English Sheepdogs, Australian Shepherds, etc., are extremely sensitive to ivermectin.

Ivermectin injections have killed some dogs, but dogs heavily infected with skin disorders may be treated anyway with small doses.

The ivermectin reaction is a toxicosis which causes tremors, loss of power to move their muscles, prolonged dilatation of the pupil of the eye, coma (unconsciousness), or cessation of breathing (death).

The toxicosis usually starts from 4-6 hours after ingestion, or as late as 12 hours. The longer it takes to set in, the milder is the reaction.

Ivermectin should only be prescribed and administered by a vet.

Some ivermectin treatments require two doses.

about six times a day, the dog loses blood from each detachment, possibly causing iron-deficiency anaemia. They are easily purged from the dog with many medications, the best of which seems to be ivermectin.

Hookworms rarely infect dogs in Britain unless they have access to grasslands.

TAPEWORMS

There are many species of tapeworms. They are carried by fleas! The dog eats the flea and thus starts the tapeworm cycle. Humans can also be infected with

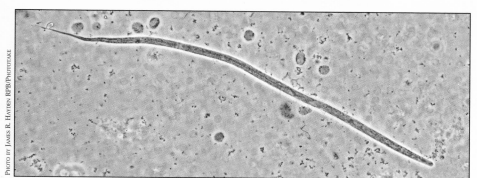

The heartworm, *Dirofilaria immitis.*

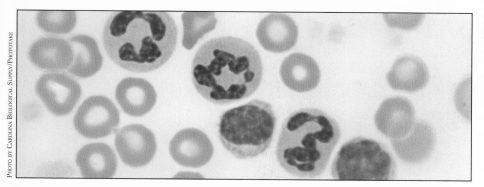

Magnified heartworm larvae, *Dirofilaria immitis.*

This surgically opened dog's heart is infected with canine heartworm, *Dirofilaria immitis.*

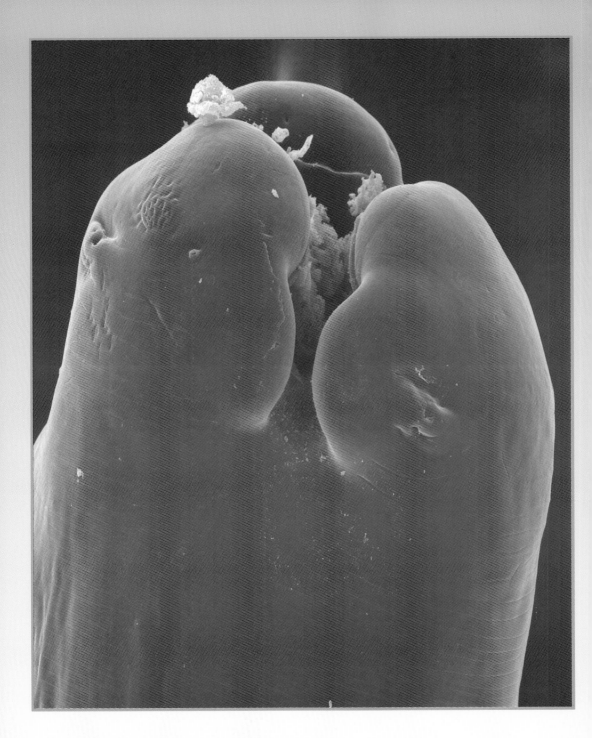

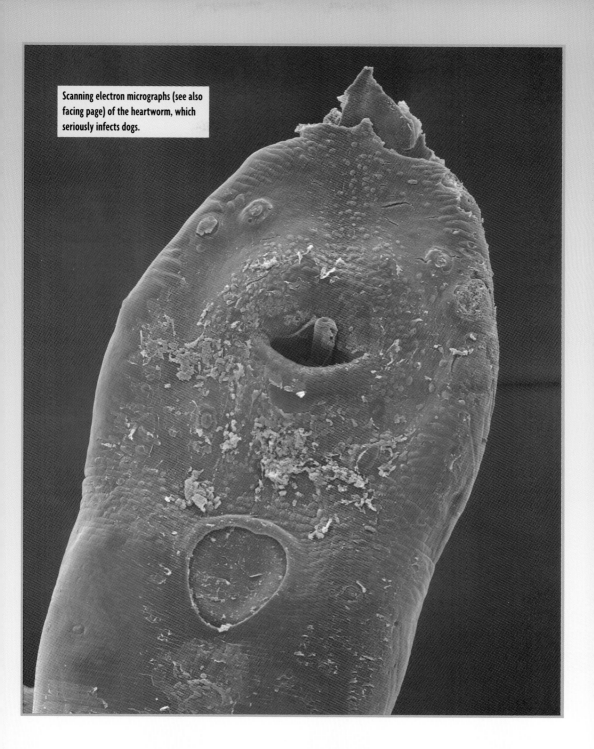

Scanning electron micrographs (see also facing page) of the heartworm, which seriously infects dogs.

DID YOU KNOW?

Flea-killers are poisonous. You should not spray these toxic chemicals on areas of the dog's body that he licks, on his genitals or on his face. Flea-killers taken internally are a better answer, but check with your vet in case internal therapy is not advised for your dog.

up to 200 of these worms. The symptoms may be loss of energy, loss of appetite, coughing, the development of a pot belly and anaemia.

Heartworms are transmitted by mosquitoes. The mosquito drinks the blood of an infected dog and takes in larvae with the blood. The larvae, called microfi-

Heartworms are very dangerous. Even though heartworms may not be found in your area, your vet may wish to include a heartworm exam in his routine physical.

tapeworms, so don't eat fleas! Fleas are so small that your dog could pass them onto your hands, your plate or your food and thus make it possible for you to ingest a flea which is carrying tapeworm eggs.

While tapeworm infection is not life threatening in dogs (smart parasite!), it can be the cause of a very serious liver disease for humans. About 50 percent of the humans infected with *Echinococcus multilocularis,* causing alveolar hydatis, perish.

Whether you have a puppy or an older dog, your children must be trained in the care and handling of a Yorkie. Yorkies are small, sensitive and dependent upon their human companions.

HEARTWORMS

Heartworms are thin, extended worms up to 30 cm (12 in.) long which live in a dog's heart and major blood vessels around the heart. Yorkshire Terriers may have

laria, develop within the body of the mosquito and are passed on to the next dog bitten after the larvae mature. It takes 2-3 weeks for the larvae to develop to the infective stage within the body of the mosquito. Dogs should be treated at about 6 weeks of age, then every 6 months.

Blood testing for heartworms is not necessarily indicative of how seriously your dog is infected. This is a dangerous disease. Dogs in the United Kingdom are not affected by heartworm.

When Your Yorkshire Terrier Gets Old

The term old is a qualitative term. For dogs, as well as their masters, old is relative. Certainly we can all distinguish between a puppy Yorkshire Terrier and an adult Yorkshire Terrier—there are the obvious physical traits such as size and appearance, and personality traits like their antics and the expressions on their faces. Puppies that are nasty are very rare. Puppies and young dogs like to play with children. Children's

DID YOU KNOW?
The bottom line is simply that a dog is getting old when YOU think it is getting old because it slows down in its general activities, including walking, running, eating, jumping and retrieving. On the other hand, certain activities increase, like more sleeping, more licking your hands and body, more barking and more repetition of habits like going to the door when you put your coat on without being called.

As your Yorkie gets older, physical and behavioral problems and changes occur. Always treat your senior with respect and special care.

You should examine your Yorkie's mouth on a regular basis, especially as the dog gets older. Report changes in gum colouration to your vet.

natural exuberance is a good match for the seemingly endless energy of young dogs. They like to run, jump, chase and retrieve. When dogs grow up and cease their interaction with children, they are often thought of as being too old to play with the kids.

On the other hand, if a Yorkshire Terrier is only exposed to people over 60 years of age, its life will normally be less active and it will not seem to be getting old as soon as its activity level slows down.

If people live to be 100 years old, dogs live to be 20 years old. While this is a good rule of thumb, it is VERY inaccurate. When trying to compare dog years to human years, you cannot make a generalisation about all dogs. You can make the generalisation that, say, 14 years is a good life span for a Yorkshire Terrier. Dogs are generally considered mature within three years. They can reproduce even earlier. So the first three years of a dog's life are more like seven times that of comparable humans. That means a three-year-old dog is like a 21-year-old person. As the curve of comparison shows, there is no hard and fast rule for comparing dog and human ages. The comparison is made even more difficult, for not all humans age at the same rate...and human females live longer than human males.

DID YOU KNOW?

The symptoms listed below are symptoms that gradually appear and gradually become more noticeable. They are not life threatening, however, the symptoms below are to be taken very seriously and a discussion with your veterinary surgeon is warranted:

• Your dog cries and whimpers when it moves and stops running completely.

• Convulsions start or become more serious and frequent. The usual convulsion (spasm) is when the dog stiffens and starts to tremble being unable or unwilling to move. The seizure usually lasts for 5 to 30 minutes.

• More and more toilet accidents occur. Urine and bowel movements take place indoors without warning.

• Vomiting becomes more and more frequent.

WHAT TO DO WHEN THE TIME COMES
You are never fully prepared to make a rational decision about

putting your dog to sleep. It is very obvious that you love your Yorkshire Terrier or you would not be reading this book. Putting a loved dog to sleep is extremely difficult. It is a decision that must be made with your veterinary surgeon. You are usually forced to make the decision when one of the life-threatening symptoms listed above

DID YOU KNOW?

Euthanasia must be done by a licensed veterinary surgeon. There also may be societies for the prevention of cruelty to animals in your area. They often offer this service upon a vet's recommendation.

becomes serious enough for you to seek medical (veterinary) help.

If the prognosis of the malady indicates the end is near and your beloved pet will only suffer more and experience no enjoyment for the balance of its life, then there is no choice but euthanasia.

When your Yorkie stops retrieving or loses interest in physical activities, you should refrain from initiating such activities too regularly.

WHAT IS EUTHANASIA?

Euthanasia derives from the Greek meaning good death. In other words, it means the planned, pain-

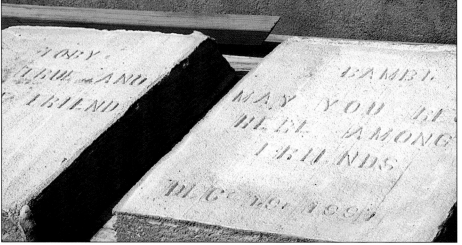

Grave stones or other grave markers are common in pet cemeteries. It is not unusual for more than one pet to be buried at the same site.

less killing of a dog suffering from a painful, incurable condition, or who is so aged that it cannot walk, see, eat or control its excretory functions.

Euthanasia is usually accomplished by injection with an over-

> **DID YOU KNOW?**
> The more open discussion you have about the whole stressful occurrence, the easier it will be for you when the time comes.

dose of an anaesthesia or barbiturate. Aside from the prick of the needle, the experience is painless.

HOW ABOUT YOU?
The days during which the dog becomes ill and the end occurs can be unusually stressful for you.

If this is your first experience with the death of a loved one, you may need the comfort dictated by your religious beliefs. If you are the head of the family and have children, you should have involved them in the decision of putting your Yorkshire Terrier to sleep. In any case, euthanasia alone is painful and stressful for the family of the dog. Unfortunately, it does not

end there. The decision-making process is just as hard.

Usually your dog can be maintained on drugs for a few days while it is kept in the clinic in order to give you ample time to make a decision. During this time, talking with members of the family or religious representatives, or even people who have lived through this same experience, can ease the burden of your inevitable decision...but then what?

How About the Final Resting Place?

Dogs can have the same privileges as humans. They can be buried in their entirety in a pet cemetery (very expensive) in a burial container, buried in your garden in a place suitably marked with a stone or newly planted tree or bush, cremated with the ashes being given to you, or even stuffed and mounted by a taxidermist.

All of these options should be discussed frankly and openly with your veterinary surgeon. Do not be afraid to ask financial questions. Cremations are usually mass burning and the ashes you get may not be the ashes of your beloved dog. There are very small crematoriums available to all veterinary clinics. If you want a private cremation, your vet can usually arrange it. However, this may be a little more expensive.

Getting Another Dog?

The grief of losing your beloved dog will be as lasting as the grief of losing a human friend or relative. You cannot go out and buy another grandfather, but you can

The loss of a faithful and beloved pet is difficult to handle.

go out and buy another Yorkshire Terrier. In most cases, if your dog died of old age (if there is such a thing), it had slowed down considerably. Do you want a new Yorkshire Terrier puppy to replace it? Or are you better off in finding a more mature Yorkshire Terrier, say two to three years of age, which will usually be house-trained and will have an already

As your Yorkie gets older, he still wants love and attention. Perhaps even more so!

developed personality. In this case, you can find out if you like each other after a few hours of being together.

The decision is, of course, your own. Do you want another Yorkshire Terrier? Perhaps you want a larger dog? How much do you want to spend on a dog? Look in your local newspapers for advertisements (DOGS FOR SALE), or, better yet, consult your local society for the prevention of cruelty to animals to adopt a dog. You may be able to find another Yorkshire Terrier, or you may choose another breed or a mixed-breed dog. It is harder to find pup-

pies at an animal shelter, but there are often many adult dogs in need of new homes. Private dog kennels specialising in a particular breed are the source for high-quality dogs that they usually breed from champion stock.

Whatever you decide, do it as quickly as possible. Most people usually buy the same breed they had before because they know (and love) the characteristics of that breed. Then, too, they often know people who have the same breed and perhaps they are lucky enough that one of their friends expects a litter soon. What could be better?

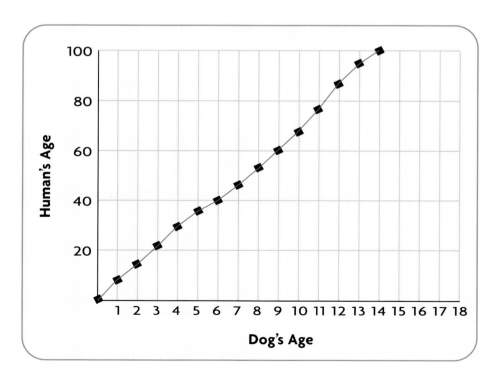

CDS: COGNITIVE DYSFUNCTION SYNDROME
"Old-Dog Syndrome"

There are many ways to evaluate old-dog syndrome. Veterinary surgeons have defined CDS (cognitive dysfunction syndrome) as the gradual deterioration of cognitive abilities. These are indicated by changes in the dog's behaviour. When a dog changes its routine response, and maladies have been eliminated as the cause of these behavioural changes, then CDS is the usual diagnosis.

More than half the dogs over 8 years old suffer some form of CDS. The older the dog, the more chance it has of suffering from CDS. In humans, doctors often dismiss the CDS behavioural changes as part of 'winding down.'

There are four major signs of CDS: frequent toilet accidents inside the home, sleeps much more or much less than normal, acts confused, and fails to respond to social stimuli.

SYMPTOMS OF CDS

FREQUENT TOILET ACCIDENTS
- *Urinates in the house.*
- *Defecates in the house.*
- *Doesn't signal that he wants to go out.*

SLEEP PATTERNS
- *Moves much more slowly.*
- *Sleeps more than normal during the day.*
- *Sleeps less during the night.*
- *Walks around listlessly and without a destination goal.*

CONFUSION
- *Goes outside and just stands there.*
- *Appears confused with a faraway look in his eyes.*
- *Hides more often.*
- *Doesn't recognise friends.*
- *Doesn't come when called.*

FAILS TO RESPOND TO SOCIAL STIMULI
- *Comes to people less frequently, whether called or not.*
- *Doesn't tolerate petting for more than a short time.*
- *Doesn't come to the door when you return home from work.*

Your show Yorkie loves to be dressed up for the big event. Grooming is the major effort in dog show participation as Yorkies must be carefully groomed for showing and it takes effort on your part to learn how to groom and to keep at it on a daily basis.

Showing Your Yorkshire Terrier

Is the puppy you selected growing into a handsome representative of his breed? You are rightly proud of your handsome little tyke, and he has mastered nearly all of the basic obedience commands that you have taught him. How about attending a dog show and seeing how the other half of the dog-loving world lives! Even if you never imagined yourself standing in the centre ring at the Crufts Dog Show, why not dream a little?

The first concept that the canine novice learns when watching a dog show is that each breed first competes against members of its own breed. Once the judge has selected the best member of each breed, then that chosen dog will compete with other dogs in its group. Finally the best of each group will compete for Best in Show and Reserve Best in Show.

The second concept that you must understand is that the dogs are not actually competing with one another. The judge compares each dog against the breed standard, which is a written description of the ideal specimen of the breed. This imaginary dog never

Breeders attempt to get as close to the ideal as possible.

walked into a show ring, has never been bred and, to the woe of dog breeders around the globe, does not exist. Breeders attempt to get as close to this ideal as possible, with every litter, but theoreti-

A Yorkie's conformation to the standard has no bearing on its quality as a pet. The grooming of pet dogs is less involved and time-consuming than the meticulous grooming of show dogs.

If your Yorkie is of show quality, you really should explore the dog shows through your local breed club.

5694

cally the 'perfect' dog is so elusive that it is impossible. (And if the 'perfect' dog were born, breeders and judges would never agree that it was indeed 'perfect.')

If you are interested in exploring dog shows, your best bet is to join your local breed club. These clubs host shows (often matches and open shows for beginners), send out newsletters, offer training days and provide an outlet to meet members who are often friendly and generous with their

The way your Yorkie moves, his gait, is one of the criteria upon which the dog is judged.

The evaluation of your Yorkie by an experienced judge can be very enlightening.

advice and contacts. To locate the nearest breed club for you, contact The Kennel Club, the ruling body for the British dog world, not just for conformation shows, but for working trials, obedience trials, agility trials and field trials. The Kennel Club furnishes the rules and regulations for all these events plus general dog registration and other basic requirements of dog ownership. Its annual show, held in Birmingham, is the largest bench show in England. Every year no fewer than 20,000 of the U.K.'s best dogs qualify to participate in a marvelous show lasting four days.

In shows held under the auspices of The Kennel Club, which includes Great Britain, Australia, South Africa and beyond, there are different kinds of shows. At the most competitive and prestigious of these shows, the

Championship Shows, a dog can earn Challenge Certificates, and thereby become a 'champion.' A dog must earn three Challenge Certificates under three different judges to earn the prefix of 'Sh Ch.' or 'Ch.' Note that some breeds must qualify in a field trial in order to gain the title of full champion. Challenge Certificates are awarded to a very small percentage of the dogs competing, and the number of Challenge Certificates awarded in any one year is based upon the total number of dogs in each breed entered for competition. There are three types of Championship Shows, a general show, where all breeds recognised by The Kennel Club can enter, a Group show, and a breed show, which is limited to only a single breed.

Open Shows are generally less competitive and are frequently used as 'practice shows' for young dogs. These shows, of which there are hundreds each year, can be invitingly social events and are great first show experiences for the novice. If you're just considering watching a show to wet your paws, an Open Show is a great choice.

While Championship and Open Shows are most important for the beginner to understand, there are other types of shows in which the interested dog owner can participate. Training clubs, for example, sponsor Matches

This wind-blown show dog has the appearance of a well-trained contender. With dedication, patience and experience, you can show and win with your Yorkie at a conformation event.

Dog shows are fun as well as educational. You can expect to meet a lot of nice people in the show dog circuit.

that can be entered on the day of the show for a nominal fee. These introductory level exhibitions are uniquely run: two dogs are pulled from a raffle and 'matched,' the winner of that match goes on to the next round, and eventually only one dog is left undefeated.

Exemption shows are similar in that they are simply fun classes and usually held in conjunction with small agricultural

HOW TO ENTER A DOG SHOW

1. Obtain an entry form and show schedule from the Show Secretary.
2. Select the classes that you want to enter and complete the entry form.
3. Transfer your dog into your name at The Kennel Club. (Be sure that this matter is handled before entering.)
4. Find out how far in advance show entries must be made. Oftentimes it's more than a couple of months.

145

Setting your Yorkshire Terrier up on his grooming bench allows the judge to better view the dog's whole body and structure. Watch a dog show to learn the 'tricks of the trade.'

shows. Primary shows can also be entered on the day of the event and dogs entered must not have won anything towards their titles. Sanction and Limited shows must be entered well in advance, and there are limitations upon who can enter. Regardless of which type show you choose to begin with, you and your dog will have a grand time competing and learning your way about the shows.

Before you actually step into the ring, you would be well advised to sit back and observe the judge's ring procedure. If it is your first time in the ring, do not be over-anxious and run to

DID YOU KNOW?

Just like with anything else, there is a certain etiquette to the show ring that can only be learned through experience. Showing your dog can be quite intimidating to you as a novice when it seems as if everyone else knows what he's doing. You can familiarise yourself with ring procedure beforehand by taking a class to prepare you and your dog for conformation showing or by talking with an experienced handler. When you are in the ring, listen and pay attention to the judge and follow his/her directions. Remember, even the most skilled handlers had to start somewhere. Keep it up and you too will be a pro in no time!

the front of the line. It is much better when you can stand back and study how the exhibitor in front of you is performing. The judge asks each handler to 'stand' the dog, hopefully showing the dog off to his best advantage. The judge will observe the dog from a distance and from different angles, approach the dog, check his teeth, overall structure, alertness and muscle tone, as well as consider how well the dog 'conforms' to the standard. Most importantly, the judge will have the exhibitor move the dog around the ring in

WORKING TRIALS

Working trials can be entered by any well-trained dog of any breed, not just Gundogs or Working dogs. Many dogs that earn the Kennel Club Good Citizen Dog award choose to participate in a working trial. There are five stakes at both open and

A Crufts winner is all smiles! There is hardly a more pleasuresome experience for a Yorkie owner than winning at the greatest of all dog shows.

Every part of the Yorkshire Terrier must be groomed for the show ring.

some pattern that he or she should specify (another advantage to not going first, but always listen since some judges change their directions, and the judge is always right!) Finally the judge will give the dog one last look before moving on to the next exhibitor.

If you are not in the top three at your first show, do not be discouraged. Be patient and consistent and you will eventually find yourself in the winning lineup. Remember that the winners were once in your shoes and have devoted many hours and much money to earn the placement. If you find that your dog is losing every time and never getting a nod, it may be time to consider a different dog sport or just to enjoy your Yorkshire Terrier as a pet.

championship levels: Companion Dog (CD), Utility Dog (UD), Working Dog (WD), Tracking Dog (TD), and Patrol Dog (PD). Like in conformation shows, dogs compete against a standard and if the dog reaches the qualifying mark, it obtains a certificate. Divided into groups,

WINNING THE TICKET

Earning a championship at Kennel Club shows is the most difficult in the world. Compared to the United States and Canada where it is relatively not 'challenging,' collecting three green tickets not only requires much time and effort, it can be very expensive! Challenge Certificates, as the tickets are properly known, are the building blocks of champions— good breeding, good handling, good training and good luck!

each exercise must be achieved 70 percent in order to qualify. If the dog achieves 80 percent in the open level, it receives a Certificate of Merit (COM), in the championship level, it receives a Qualifying Certificate. At the CD stake, dogs must participate in four groups, Control, Stay, Agility and Search (Retrieve and Nosework). At the next three levels, UD, WD and TD, there are only three groups: Control, Agility and Nosework.

Agility consists of three jumps: a vertical scale up a wall of planks; a clear jump over a basic hurdle with a removable top bar; and a long jump of angled planks.

To earn the UD, WD and TD, dogs must track approximately one-half mile for articles laid from one-half hour to three hours ago. Tracks consist of turns and legs, and fresh ground is used for each participant.

The fifth stake, PD, involves teaching manwork, which of course is not recommended for every breed.

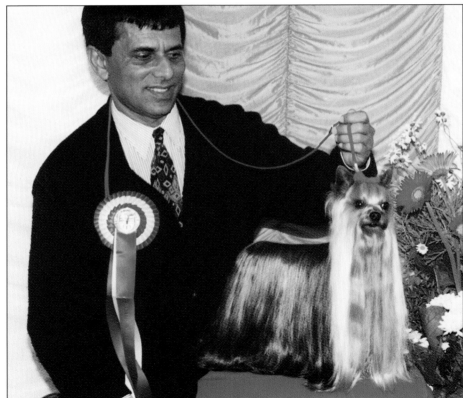

Ch Ozmilion Mystification, owned and handled by Osman Sameja, was the first Yorkshire Terrier to win Best in Show at Crufts. 'Justin' was the winner of 50 CCs and 12 BISs.

A champion-quality Yorkie, perfectly groomed, is a pleasing spectacle.

Crufts
BEST IN SHOW

AGILITY TRIALS

Agility trials began in the United Kingdom in 1977 and have since spread around the world, especially to the United States, where it enjoys strong popularity. The handler directs his dog over an obstacle course that includes jumps (such as those used in the working trials), as well as tyres, the dog walk, weave poles, pipe tunnels, collapsed tunnels, etc. The Kennel Club requires that dogs not be trained for agility until they are 12 months old. This dog sport intends to be great fun for dog and owner and interested owners should join a training club that has obstacles and experienced agility handlers who can introduce you and your dog to the 'ropes' (and tyres, tunnels and so on).

Yorkies are groomed to the last minute before being presented to the judge. The patient Yorkie endures his handler's stroking until the final moment of truth.

(opposite page) It just does not get any better than this: Best in Show at Crufts in 1997. Ch Ozmilion Mystification retired after this victory. In 1996 he was the Top Dog in England.

FÉDÉRATION CYNOLOGIQUE INTERNATIONALE

Established in 1911, the Fédération Cynologique Internationale represents the 'world kennel club,' the international body brings uniformity to

DID YOU KNOW?

You can get information about dog shows from kennel clubs and breed clubs:

Fédération Cynologique Internationale
14, rue Leopold II, B-6530 Thuin, Belgium

The Kennel Club
1-5 Clarges St., Piccadilly, London W1Y 8AB, UK
www.the-kennel-club.org.uk

American Kennel Club
5580 Centerview Dr., Raleigh, NC 27606-3390, USA
www.akc.org

Canadian Kennel Club
89 Skyway Ave., Suite 100, Etobicoke, Ontario M9W 6R4 Canada
www.ckc.ca

The Yorkshire Terrier is a most impressionable dog. The handler's nervous state and insecurities can affect the dog's performance.

MADISON SQUARE GARDEN CENTER
Seventh to Eighth Aves. & 31st to 33rd Streets, New York City

123rd ANNUAL DOG SHOW
THE WESTMINSTER KENNEL CLUB
MONDAY and TUESDAY, FEBRUARY 8 and 9, 1999

EXHIBITOR

NOT VALID UNLESS SIGNED

NOTICE Always, upon leaving this show, if you wish to return the same day, present this Ticket at Exhibitor Entrance and obtain a Return Check. This Ticket without a Return Check or Return Check without this Ticket is not good for Admission.

TUES. FEB. 9
Nº 2695 2
EXHIBITOR
MADISON SQUARE GARDEN CENTER
123rd ANNUAL DOG SHOW
THE WESTMINSTER KENNEL CLUB

MON. FEB. 8
Nº 2695 1
EXHIBITOR
MADISON SQUARE GARDEN CENTER
123rd ANNUAL DOG SHOW
THE WESTMINSTER KENNEL CLUB

The Yorkshire puppy can grow to become the adult that the owner chooses. Given exposure to proper training and experience, your Yorkie can become a star show dog or an agility trial ace.

the breeding, judging and showing of purebred dogs. Although the FCI originally included only European nations, namely France, Holland, Austria and Belgium, the latter of which remains the headquarters, the organisation today embraces nations on six continents and recognises well over 300 breeds

The glamourous life can be very trying on the Yorkshire Terrier. Even show dogs need to lie back and let their hair down!

smiles at its human friends. It never smiles at another dog or cat. Usually it rolls up its lips and shows its teeth in a clenched mouth while it rolls over onto its back begging for a soft scratch.

of purebred dog. There are three titles attainable through the FCI: the International Champion, which is the most prestigious; the International Beauty Champion, which is based on aptitude certificates in different countries; and the International Trial Champion, which is based on achievement in obedience trials in different countries. Of course, quarantine laws in

An International Beauty Champion is unmistakable. Although the standards vary from country to country, showmanship and dignity are rewarded at all shows.

England and Australia prohibit most exhibitors from entering FCI shows, though the rest of the European nations do participate in these impressive canine spectacles, the largest of which is the World Dog Show, hosted in a different country each year. FCI sponsors both national and international shows. The hosting country determines the judging system and breed standards are always based on the breed's country of origin.

Understanding Your Dog's Behaviour

As a Yorkshire Terrier owner, you have selected your dog so that you and your loved ones can have a companion, a protector, a friend and a four-legged family member. You invest time, money and effort to care for and train the family's new charge. Of course, this chosen canine behaves perfectly! Well, perfectly like a dog.

THINK LIKE A DOG

Dogs do not think like humans, nor do humans think like dogs, though we try. Unfortunately, a dog is incapable of figuring out

(opposite page) Yorkies and children seem to understand each other very well. Many trainers admit that everything they know about parenting they learned from their dogs!

how humans think, so the responsibility falls on the owner to adopt a proper canine mindset. Dogs cannot rationalise, and dogs exist in the present moment. Many dog owners make the mistake in training of thinking that they can reprimand their dog for something he did a while ago. Basically, you cannot even reprimand a dog for something he did 20 seconds ago! Either catch him in the act or forget it! It is a waste of your and your dog's time—in his mind, you are reprimanding him for whatever he is doing at that moment.

The following behavioural problems represent some which owners most commonly encounter. Every dog is unique and every situation is unique.

Your Yorkie is awaiting your arrival home. You determine how you wish for your Yorkie to greet you upon returning home. Dogs that jump up can be a nuisance to visitors to your home.

157

No author could purport to solve your Yorkshire Terrier's problem simply by reading a script. Here we outline some basic 'dogspeak' so that owners' chances of solving behavioural problems are increased. Discuss bad habits with your veterinary surgeon and he/she can recommend a behavioural specialist to consult in appropriate cases. Since behavioural abnormalities are the leading reason owners abandon their pets, we hope that you will make a valiant effort to solve your Yorkshire Terrier's problem. Patience and understanding are virtues that dwell in every pet-loving household.

AGGRESSION
Aggression can be a very big problem in dogs, not just big dogs! Aggression, when not controlled, becomes dangerous. An aggressive dog, no matter the size, may lunge at, bite or even attack a person or another dog. Aggressive behaviour is not to be tolerated. It is more than just inappropriate behaviour; it is not safe, even with a diminutive breed such as the Yorkshire Terrier. It is painful for a family to watch their dog become unpredictable in his behaviour to the point where they are afraid of the dog. And while not all aggressive behaviour is dangerous, it can be frightening: growling, baring teeth, etc. It is important to get to the root of the problem to ascertain why the dog is acting in this manner. Aggression is a display of dominance, and the dog should not have the dominant role in its pack, which is, in this case, your family.

It is important not to challenge an aggressive dog as this could provoke an attack. Observe your Yorkshire Terrier's body language. Does he make direct eye contact and stare? Does he try to make himself as large as possible: ears pricked, chest out, tail erect? Height and size signify authority in a dog pack—being taller or 'above' another dog literally means that he is 'above' in the social status. These body signals tell you that your Yorkshire Terrier thinks he is in charge, a problem that needs to be dealt with. An aggressive dog is unpredictable in that you never know when he is going to strike and what he is going to do. You cannot understand why a dog that is playful and loving one minute is growling and snapping the next.

The best solution is to consult a behavioural specialist, one who has experience with the Yorkshire Terrier if possible. Together, perhaps you can pinpoint the cause of your dog's aggression and do something about it. An aggressive dog can-

The puppy that receives proper socialisation and instruction at the breeder's is more accepting of other dogs throughout its life.

not be trusted, and a dog that cannot be trusted is not safe to have as a family pet. If the pet Yorkshire Terrier becomes untrustworthy, he cannot be kept in the home with the family. The family must get rid of the dog. In the worst case, the dog must be euthanised.

AGGRESSION TOWARD OTHER DOGS
A dog's aggressive behaviour toward another dog stems from not enough exposure to other dogs at an early age. If other dogs make your Yorkshire Terrier nervous and agitated, he will lash out as a protective mechanism. A dog who has not received sufficient exposure to other canines tends to believe that he is the only dog on the planet. The animal becomes so dominant that he does not even show signs that he is fearful or threatened. Without growling or any other physical signal as a

NAPOLEAN COMPLEX?

It is not natural for Yorkshire Terriers to act aggressively towards all other dogs. The diminutive stature of the Yorkshire Terrier of course sets the

breed at a disadvantage, even though dogs are not 'size conscious.' A Yorkshire Terrier that has not been properly socialised with other dogs, or who has become spoiled as an 'only dog,' may indeed act poorly around other dogs. Generally, Yorkies are gregarious dogs that like the company of other friendly dogs whom they know.

against when he sets about training a dog. In training a dog to obey commands, the owner is reinforcing that he is the top dog in the 'pack' and that the dog should, and should want to, serve his superior. Thus, the owner is suppressing the dog's urge to dominate by modifying his behaviour and making him obedient.

An important part of training is taking every opportunity to reinforce that you are the leader. The simple action of making

Start with a young puppy and be sure that he understands who is boss! Yorkies learn very quickly how they can train you. A cry, a whimper, a whine, a bark..all of these elicit some response from you.

warning, he will lunge at and bite the other dog. A way to correct this is to let your Yorkshire Terrier approach another dog when walking on lead. Watch very closely and at the very first sign of aggression, correct your Yorkshire Terrier and pull him away. Scold him for any sign of discomfort, and then praise him when he ignores or tolerates the other dog. Keep this up until either he stops the aggressive behaviour, learns to ignore the other dog or even accepts other dogs. Praise him lavishly for his correct behaviour.

DOMINANT AGGRESSION
A social hierarchy is firmly established in a wild dog pack. The dog wants to dominate those under him and please those above him. Dogs know that there must be a leader. If you are not the obvious choice for emperor, the dog will assume the throne! These conflicting innate desires are what a dog owner is up

ture. Dog training is not about being cruel or feeling important, it is about moulding the dog's behaviour into what is acceptable and teaching him to live by your rules. In theory, it is quite simple: catch him in appropriate behaviour and reward him for it. Add a dog into the equation and it becomes a bit more trying, but as a rule of thumb, positive reinforcement is what works best.

Exposing your Yorkie to different environment and people helps to socialise the dog. Since Yorkies must be brushed every day, you can practice this ritual in different places to nurture trust and confidence from your dog.

your Yorkshire Terrier sit to wait for his food instead of allowing him to run up to get it when he wants it says that you control when he eats; he is dependent on you for food. Although it may be difficult, do not give in to your dog's wishes every time he whines at you or looks at you with pleading eyes. It is a constant effort to show the dog that his place in the pack is at the bottom. This is not meant to sound cruel or inhumane. You love your Yorkshire Terrier and you should treat him with care and affection. You (hopefully) did not get a dog just so you could boss around another crea-

DID YOU KNOW?

When a dog bites there is always a good reason for it doing so. Many dogs are trained to protect a person, an area or an object. When that person, area or object is violated the dog will attack. A dog attacks with its mouth. It has no other means of attack. It never uses teeth for defense. It merely runs away or lays down on the ground when it is in an indefensible situation. Fighting dogs (and there are many breeds which fight) are taught to fight, but they also have a natural instinct to fight. This instinct is normally reserved for other dogs, though unfortunate accidents occur when babies crawl towards a fighting dog and the dog mistakes the crawling child as a potential attacker.

If a dog is a biter for no reason; if it bites the hand that feeds it; if it snaps at members of your family. See your veterinarian immediately for behavioural modification treatments.

DID YOU KNOW?

Punishment is rarely necessary for a misbehaving dog. Dogs that are habitually bad probably had a poor education and they do not know what is expected of them. They need training. Disciplinary behaviour on your part usually does more harm than good.

With a dominant dog, punishment and negative reinforcement can have the opposite effect of what you are after. It can make a dog fearful and/or act out aggressively if he feels he is being challenged. Remember, a dominant dog perceives himself at the top of the social heap, and will fight to defend his perceived status. The best way to prevent that is to never give him reason to think that he is in control in the first place. If you are having trouble training your Yorkshire Terrier and it seems as if he is constantly challenging your authority, seek the help of an obedience trainer or behavioural specialist. A professional will work with both you and your dog to teach you effective techniques to use at home. Beware of trainers who rely on excessively harsh methods; scolding is necessary now and then, but the focus in your training should always be on positive reinforcement.

If you can isolate what brings out the fear reaction, you can help the dog get over it. Supervise your Yorkshire Terrier's interactions with people and other dogs, and praise the dog when it goes well. If he starts to act aggressively in a situation, correct him and remove him from the situation. Do not let people approach the dog and start petting him without your express permission. That way, you can have the dog sit to accept petting, and praise him when he behaves properly. You are focusing on praise and on modifying his behaviour by rewarding him when he acts appropriately. By being gentle and by supervising his interactions, you are showing him that there is no need to be afraid or defensive.

SEXUAL BEHAVIOUR

Dogs exhibit certain sexual behaviours that may have influenced your choice of male or female when you first purchased your Yorkshire Terrier. Spaying/neutering will eliminate these behav-

DID YOU KNOW?

Your dog inherited the pack-leader mentality. He only knows about pecking order. He instinctively wants to be top dog but you have to convince him that you are boss. There is no such thing as living in a democracy with your dog. You are the dictator, the absolute monarch.

iours, but if you are purchasing a dog that you wish to breed, you should be aware of what you will have to deal with throughout the dog's life.

Female dogs usually have two oestruses per year, each season lasting about three weeks. These are the only times in which a female dog will mate, and she usually will not allow this until the second week of the cycle. If a bitch is not bred during the heat cycle, it is not uncommon for her to experience a false pregnancy, in which her mammary glands swell and she exhibits maternal tendencies toward toys or other objects.

Owners must further recognise that mounting is not merely a sexual expression but also one of dominance. Be consistent and persistent and you will find that you can 'move mounters.'

CHEWING
The national canine pastime is chewing! Every dog loves to sink his 'canines' into a tasty bone, but sometimes that bone is attached to his owner's hand! Dogs need to chew, to massage their gums, to make their new teeth feel better and to exercise their jaws. This is a natural behaviour deeply imbedded in all things canine. Our role as owners is not to stop chewing, but to redirect it to positive, chew-worthy objects. Be an informed owner and purchase proper chew toys for your Yorkshire Terrier, like nylon bones made for small dogs. Be sure that the devices are safe and durable, since your dog's safety is at risk. Again, the owner is responsible for ensuring a dog-proof environment. The best

answer is prevention: that is, put your shoes, handbags and other tasty objects in their proper places (out of the reach of the growing canine mouth). Direct puppies to their toys whenever you see them tasting the furniture legs or your trouser leg. Make a loud noise to attract the pup's attention and immediately escort him to his chew toy and engage him with the toy for at least four minutes, praising and encouraging him all the while.

DID YOU KNOW?
Never scream, shout, jump or run about if you want your dog to stay calm. You set the example for your dog's behaviour in most circumstances. Learn from your dog's reaction to your behaviour and act accordingly.

Some trainers recommend deterrents, such as hot pepper or another bitter spice or a product designed for this purpose, to discourage the dog from chewing on unwanted objects. This is sometimes reliable, though not as often as the manufacturers of such products claim. Test out the product with your own dog before investing in a case of it.

DID YOU KNOW?
Barking is your dog's way of protecting you. If he barks at a stranger walking past your house, a moving car or a fleeing cat, he is merely exercising his responsibility to protect his pack (YOU) and territory from a perceived intruder. Since the 'intruder' usually keeps going, the dog thinks his barking chased it away and he feels fulfilled. This behaviour leads your overly vocal friend to believe that he is the 'dog in charge'.

JUMPING UP
Jumping up is a dog's friendly way of saying hello! Some dog owners do not mind when their dog jumps up, which is fine for them. The problem arises when guests come to the house and the dog greets them in the same manner—whether they like it or not! However friendly the greeting may be, chances are your visitors will not appreciate being jumped up on by your Yorkshire Terrier. The dog will not be able to distin-

guish upon whom he can jump and whom he cannot. Therefore, it is probably best to discourage this behaviour entirely.

Pick a command such as 'off' (avoid using 'down' since you will use that for the dog to lie down) and tell him 'off' when he jumps up. Place him on the ground on all fours and have

If only Yorkies could remain precious little dolls, owners wouldn't need manuals about behavioural modification or professional consultants to rely upon.

165

DID YOU KNOW?

Dogs left alone for varying lengths of time may often react wildly when you return. Sometimes they run, jump, bite, chew, tear things apart, wet themselves, gobble their food or behave in a very undisciplined manner. Allow them to calm down before greeting them or they will consider your attention as a reward for their antics.

him sit, praising him the whole time. Always lavish him with praise and petting when he is in the 'sit' position. That way you are still giving him a warm affectionate greeting, because you are as excited to see him as he is to see you!

DIGGING

Digging, which is seen as a destructive behaviour to humans, is actually quite a natural behaviour in dogs. Whether or not your dog is one of the 'earth dogs' (also known as terriers), his desire to dig can be irrepressible and most frustrating to his owners. When digging occurs in your garden, it is actually a normal behaviour redirected into something the dog can do in his everyday life. For example, in the wild a dog would be actively seeking food,

making his own shelter, etc. He would be using his paws in a purposeful manner; he would be using them for his survival. Since you provide him with food and shelter, he has no need to use his paws for these purposes, and so the energy that he would be using manifests itself in the form of little holes all over your garden and flower beds.

Perhaps your dog is digging as a reaction to boredom—it is somewhat similar to someone eating a whole bag of pretzels in front of the TV—because they are there and there is not anything better to do! Basically, the answer is to provide the dog with adequate play and exercise so that his mind and paws are occupied, and so that he feels as if he is doing something useful.

DID YOU KNOW?

The number of dogs who suffer from separation anxiety is on the rise as more and more pet owners find themselves at work all day. New attention is being paid to this problem, which is especially hard to diagnose since it is only evident when the dog is alone. Research is currently being done to help educate dog owners about separation anxiety and about how they can help minimise this problem in their dogs.

Of course, digging is easiest to control if it is stopped as soon as possible, but it is often hard to catch a dog in the act, especially if he is alone in the garden during the day. If your dog is a compulsive digger and is not easily distracted by other activities, you can designate an area on your property where it is okay for him to dig. If you catch him digging in an off-limits area of the garden, immediately bring him to the approved area and praise him for digging there. Keep a close eye on him so that you can catch him, that is the only way he is going to understand what is permitted and what is not. If you bring him to a hole he dug an hour ago and tell him 'No,' he will understand that you are not fond of holes, or dirt, or flowers. If you catch him while he is stifle-deep in your tulips, that is when he will get your message.

BARKING

Dogs cannot talk—oh, what they would say if they could! Instead, barking is a dog's way of 'talking.' It can be somewhat frustrating because it is not always easy to tell what a dog means by his bark—is he excited, happy, frightened, angry? Whatever it is that the dog is trying to say, he should not be punished for barking. It is only when the barking becomes excessive, and when

> **DID YOU KNOW?**
> Dog aggression is a serious problem. NEVER give an aggressive dog to someone else. The dog will usually be more aggressive in a new situation where his leadership is unchallenged and unquestioned (in his mind).

the excessive barking becomes a bad habit, does the behaviour need to be modified. If an intruder came into your home in the middle of the night and the dog barked a warning, wouldn't you be pleased? You would probably deem your dog a hero, a wonderful guardian and protector of the home. On the other hand, if a friend drops by unexpectedly and rings the doorbell and is greeted with a sudden sharp bark, you would probably be annoyed at the dog. But isn't it just the same behaviour? The dog does not know any better... unless he sees who is at the door and it is someone he is familiar with, he will bark as a means of vocalising that his (and your) territory is being threatened. While your friend is not posing a threat, it is all the same to the dog. Barking is his means of letting you know that there is an intrusion, whether friend or foe, on your property. This type of barking is instinctive and should not be discouraged.

DID YOU KNOW?

If you are approached by an aggressive, growling dog, do not run away. Simply stand still and avoid eye contact. If you have something in your hand (like a handbag), throw it sideways away from your body to distract the dog from making a frontal attack.

Excessive habitual barking, however, is a problem that should be corrected early on. As your Yorkshire Terrier grows up, you will be able to tell when his barking is purposeful and when it is for no reason. You will become able to distinguish your dog's different barks and with what they are associated. For example, the bark when someone comes to the door will be different from the bark when he is excited to see you. It is similar to a person's tone of voice, except that the dog has to rely totally on tone of voice because he does not have the benefit of using words. An incessant barker will be evident at an early age.

There are some things that encourage a dog to bark. For example, if your dog barks non-stop for a few minutes and you give him a treat to quieten him, he believes that you are rewarding him for barking. He will associate barking with getting a treat, and will keep doing it until he is rewarded.

FOOD STEALING

Is your dog devising ways of stealing food from the cubboard? If so, you must answer the following questions: Is your Yorkshire Terrier hungry, or is he 'constantly famished' like every other chow hound? Why is there food on the coffee table? Face it, some dogs are more food-motivated than others; some dogs are totally obsessed by a slab of brisket and can only think of their next meal. Food stealing is terrific fun and always yields a great reward— FOOD, glorious food.

The owner's goal, therefore, is to make the 'reward' less rewarding, even startling! Plant a shaker can (an empty pop can with coins inside) on the counter so that it catches your pooch off-guard. There are other devices available that will surprise the dog when he is looking for a mid-afternoon snack. Such remote-control devices, though not the first choice of some trainers, allow the correction to come from the object instead of the owner. These devices are also useful to keep the snacking pooch from napping on furniture that is forbidden.

BEGGING

Just like food stealing, begging is a favourite pastime of hungry puppies! With that same reward—FOOD! Dogs quickly learn that their owners keep the 'good food' for themselves, and that we humans do not dine on kibble alone. Begging is a conditioned response related to a specific stimulus, time and place. The sounds of the kitchen, cans and bottles opening, crinkling bags, the smell of food in preparation, etc., will excite the chow hound and soon the paws are in the air!

Here is the solution to stopping this behaviour: Never give into a beggar! You are rewarding the dog for sitting pretty, jumping up, whining and rubbing his nose into you by giving him that glorious reward—food. By ignoring the dog, you will (eventually) force the behaviour into extinction. Note that the behaviour likely gets worse before it disappears, so be sure there are not any 'softies' in the family who will give in to little 'Oliver' every time he whimpers, 'More, please.'

SEPARATION ANXIETY

Your Yorkshire Terrier may howl, whine or otherwise vocalise his displeasure at your leaving the house and his being left alone. This is a normal case of separation anxiety, but there are things that can be done to eliminate this problem. Your dog needs to learn that he will be fine on his own for a while and that he will not wither away if he is not attended to every minute of the day. In fact, constant attention can lead to separation anxiety in the first place. If you are endlessly coddling and cooing over your dog, he will come to expect this from you all of the time and it will be

Few dogs are as dependent upon their masters as the Yorkshire Terrier. Leaving a Yorkie alone for hours on end is very stressful on the dog and may lead to behavioural and health problems.

more traumatic for him when you are not there. Obviously, you enjoy spending time with your dog, and he thrives on your love and attention. However, it should not become a dependent relationship where he is heart-broken without you.

One thing you can do to minimise separation anxiety is to make your entrances and exits as low-key as possible. Do not give your dog a long drawn-out good-bye, and do not lavish him with hugs and kisses when you return. This is giving in to the attention that he craves, and it will only make him miss it more when you are away. Another thing you can try is to give your dog a treat when you leave; this will not only keep him occupied and keep his mind off the fact that you just left, but it will also

This couple loved their Yorkie so much they invited it to their wedding!

help him associate your leaving with a pleasant experience.

You may have to accustom your dog to being left alone in intervals, much like when you introduced your pup to his crate. Of course, when your dog starts whimpering as you approach the door, your first instinct will be to run to him and comfort him, but do not do it! Really—eventually he will

adjust and be just fine if you take it in small steps. His anxiety stems from being placed in an unfamiliar situation; by familiarising him with being alone he will learn that he is okay. That is not to say you should purposely leave your dog home alone, but the dog needs to know that while he can depend on you for his care, you do not have to be by his side 24 hours a day.

When the dog is alone in the house, he should be confined to his crate or a designated dog-proof area of the house. This should be the area in which he sleeps, so he should already feel comfortable there and this should make him feel more at ease when he is alone. This is just one of the many examples in which a crate is an invaluable tool for you and your dog, and another reinforcement of why your dog should view his crate as a 'happy' place, a place of his own.

COPROPHAGIA

Faeces eating is, to most humans, one of the most disgusting behaviours that their dog could engage in, yet to the dog it is perfectly normal. It is hard for us to understand why a dog would want to eat its own faeces; he could be seeking certain nutrients that are missing from his diet, he could be just plain hungry, or he could be attracted by the pleasing (to a dog) scent. While coprophagia most often refers to the dog eating his own faeces, a dog may likely eat that of another animal as well if he comes across it. Vets have found that diets with a low digestibility, containing relatively low levels of fibre and high levels of starch, increase coprophagia. Therefore, high-fibre diets may decrease the likelihood of dogs eating faeces. Both the consistency of the stool (how firm it feels in the dog's mouth) and the presence of undigested nutrients increase the likelihood. Dogs often find the stool of cats and horses more palatable than that of other dogs. Once the dog develops diarrhoea from faeces eating, it will likely quit this distasteful habit, since dogs tend to prefer eating harder faeces.

To discourage this behaviour, first make sure that the food you are feeding your dog is nutritionally complete and that he is getting enough food. If changes in his diet do not seem to work, and no medical cause can be found, you will have to modify the behaviour through environmental control before it becomes a habit. There are some tricks you can try, such as adding an unpleasant-tasting substance to the faeces to make them unpalatable or adding something to the dog's food which will make it unpleasant tasting after it passes

Small dogs like Yorkies are unfortunately prone to 'stool sampling.' Most outgrow this impoliteness in no time.

through the dog. The best way to prevent your dog from eating his stool is to make it unavailable—clean up after he eliminates and remove any stool from the garden. If it is not there, he cannot eat it.

Never reprimand the dog for stool eating, as this rarely impresses the dog. Vets recommend distracting the dog while he is in the act of stool eating. Coprophagia most frequently is seen in pups 6 to 12 months of age, and usually disappears around the dog's first birthday.

Owning and training a Yorkshire Terrier is rewarding for children and adults alike.

INDEX

*Page numbers in **boldface** indicate illustrations.*

My Yorkshire Terrier

PUT YOUR PUPPY'S FIRST PICTURE HERE

Dog's Name _____

Date _____ Photographer _____